EXTRA HELPING

RECIPES FOR CARING, CONNECTING & BUILDING COMMUNITY

ONE DISH AT A TIME

JANET REICH ELSBACH

PAPERCUTS BY ANNA BRONES

ROOST BOOKS   BOULDER | 2018

Roost Books
An imprint of Shambhala Publications, Inc.
4720 Walnut Street
Boulder, Colorado 80301
roostbooks.com

9 8 7 6 5 4 3 2 1

First Edition
Printed in the United States of America

⊛This edition is printed on acid-free paper that meets the American National
Standards Institute Z39.48 Standard.
♻This book is printed on 30% postconsumer recycled paper.
For more information please visit www.shambhala.com.

Roost Books is distributed worldwide by Penguin Random House, Inc. and its
subsidiaries.

Designed by Danielle Deschenes

Library of Congress Cataloging-in-Publication Data
Names: Elsbach, Janet Reich, author.
Title: Extra helping: recipes for caring, connecting, and building community one
dish at a time /
  Janet Reich Elsbach; papercuts by Anna Brones.
Description: First edition. | Boulder: Roost Books, 2018. | Includes
  bibliographical references and index.
Identifiers: LCCN 2017055626 | ISBN 9781611806021 (pbk.: acid-free paper)
Subjects: LCSH: Cooking. | LCGFT: Cookbooks.
Classification: LCC TX714 .E456 2018 | DDC 641.5—dc 3
LC record available at https://lccn.loc.gov/2017055626

FOR HAZEL, PEARL, AND ASHER.

EVERYBODY HAS THEIR REASONS,
AND YOU ARE MINE.

WE'RE ALL JUST
WALKING
EACH OTHER
HOME.

RAM DASS

CONTENTS

1

FOOD FOR EXPANDING FAMILIES

2

FOOD FOR THE REARRANGED AND RELOCATED

3

FOOD FOR ILLNESS AND RECOVERY

4

FOOD FOR SOLACE

5

FOOD FOR CHEER, DISTRACTION, AND CELEBRATION

6

FOOD FOR LUNCH BOXES AND CARE PACKAGES

7

FOOD FOR A CROWD

AFTERWORD
CARING FOR THE CAREGIVER

FOREWORD

Shortly after the presidential election in 2016, I found myself, like many people I know, uncertain about our country and eager to get more involved in my community. Like I do in all times of uncertainty, I turned to food. As a lifelong home cook and a cookbook author, food has always been my anchor. In pivoting my passion to be not only about the joy of food but also the power it has to effect change, my life changed. It became way bigger than me. I got to meet, listen to, and work with tons of new people, including all the great contributors to a book I put together called *Feed the Resistance,* and other like-minded home cooks devoted to their communities like Janet Reich Elsbach.

I first got to know Janet when she signed up to be on the food team I had started. What's a food team? Glad you asked. During the hazy time postelection, I started attending meetings at my local chapter of Citizen Action of New York, a grassroots organization with a number of offices in New York State that's committed to ensuring important things like quality education, affordable health care, and racial justice. During one of these first meetings, the lead organizer asked me what I do, and I told her I work on cookbooks. She said, "Great, you'll be part of the food team." I asked her who I should report to and she said, "You're going to run it." She helped me open my eyes to seeing that I could do what I was doing anyway—working with food—but with greater meaning and purpose.

I began reaching out to people who were interested in using food to support the organization. The list became an amazing group of home cooks from near and far who would help provide a homemade meal for many of the organization's meetings, phone banking sessions, protests, and more. The food would help to save money,

keep the volunteers fed and healthy, act as an incentive for people to show up, and also very much give the home cooks providing the food a way to stay connected without necessarily being on the frontlines. If I've learned anything since starting this work, it's that the most meaningful and productive forms of resistance are the ones that you can sustain.

Janet knows this, too. Reading through *Extra Helping*, it's clear that she understands that cooking is not just a way to support people who are doing important work, it's also an act of love. It's a tangible and meaningful way to show up not only when the country's politics are on shaky ground but also when someone nearby welcomes a new child or grieves a loved one. Cooking for someone who has just moved or is recovering from illness is one of the clearest ways to say "I'm with you." It's a way to say all the things we sometimes don't have words for.

I was so delighted when Janet first shared *Extra Helping* with me. Written with a comforting voice and full of easy-to-follow, approachable recipes, it's such a useful book to have nearby. There are recipes for all of life's occasions, from the exciting to the dreaded and everything in between.

In the "Food for Expanding Families" section, there's everything from gluten-free (but great for everyone) Cinnamon Apple Muffins to Carnitas fragrant with orange and cumin that are served with roasted sweet potatoes and corn tortillas. In the "Food for the Rearranged and Relocated" section, how could you resist Life Is Upside-Down Cake? There are soups and broths in "Food for Illness and Recovery," plus warming Congee and soothing Ginger Custard. In "Food for Solace," there are not only meatballs but also UnMeatballs. Something for everyone. In "Food for Cheer, Distraction, and Celebration," there are joyous things like tart, bright Lemon Curd and a homemade ice cream shell . . . so fun! There's also portable food for lunch boxes and care packages and great recipes for crowds, including A Cauldron of Soup. I especially love the full-circle gesture of the final section, "Caring for the Caregiver."

Janet gives us all even more ideas under the Get Active heading in the "Resources" section about ways to get involved and connected, whether it's buying bread from Hot Bread Kitchen in New York City or taking an immersive cooking class from the League of Kitchens, or supporting San Francisco's La Cocina. *Extra Helping* is a bit like teaching us how to fish rather than just giving us a fish, while also giving us lots of ideas for how to prepare the fish and think about how others are doing the same.

And icing on the cake, some of the proceeds from *Extra Helping* go to Meals on Wheels, which means that by merely purchasing this book, you've already begun to help feed people who otherwise might not have access to quality food when they need it the most.

I trust you'll get so much out of *Extra Helping*. I know I have.

Yours in the kitchen and in community,

JULIA TURSHEN,

author of *Small Victories,*
Feed the Resistance,
and *Now & Again*

INTRODUCTION

EVERYONE HAS TO EAT.

Life, and especially life in community, offers endless opportunities to hone the craft of feeding those too taxed to feed themselves, as well as the art of gracefully receiving this attention when the affected person is under your own roof (or staring back at you from the mirror).

Growing and welcoming babies, nursing them through illnesses and other insults, seeing them off to camps and schools where mail call comes but once a day, moving house, suffering losses of near and dear ones, and all the other facts of lives . . . the things we survive have one common thread: if we got through it, we must have eaten something.

The only thing that compares to the satisfaction of eating what's just right for you in a particular moment of need is the relief of not needing to explain it, or even lift a finger to make it appear. How good it feels to be fed!

I think feeding others can be just as satisfying.

Food has always been love to me. I grew up in a household where the table was the point. Cooking for and eating with friends gives shape to many of my childhood memories, and as I grew, my brain became a kind of directory of the likes and aversions of the people I love. To me, the measure of how well I know someone is just about exactly equivalent to how well I know their food preferences. If I can name the thing on a plate that makes her scoot closer to the table, if I can imagine a little treat that I know will delight him, if I know what allergy she has or which arcane childhood distaste he has toted along into adulthood, or am familiar with any other peculiarity of their appetite, then I am satisfied that I know this person. Feeding people is central to how I think about friendship all of the time, and most especially when things begin to hit the fan.

When we're in the thick of a significant challenge, basic tasks start to feel like mountain climbs, and the most basic act of all—nourishing the body—often presents as the highest peak. Regular life has given me the opportunity to offer food to friends and relations experiencing trials on a sliding scale from a bad cold to cancer, from breakups to epic losses, and I've fed loved ones celebrating the joys of new babies and other blessings. I've done other things in my life besides feed people, of course, but these edible offerings are some of the most consistently satisfying things I can recall. People are so grateful to be fed, and providing for them rewards both giver and receiver.

Accepting this kind of attention was a different kind of challenge. The birth of our second child was the first time I can recall being on the receiving end of a proper dinner bucket brigade, and being fed when you have a new baby is enough to make anyone pretty pious about meal trains. Then in a terrible run of years, life really stepped up efforts to teach me how to receive with grace. My father experienced three cancers, my middle sister two. A cancer that could not be overcome came for my oldest sister, and as we reeled from her illness and death, my father underwent a series of three brain surgeries. I racked up mile after mile going back and forth to each of the places they lived, to the places they sought treatment, and to a few places not on any map I'd ever consulted. My husband and children and I pulled through all of that intact and upright thanks to the kindness of friends, much of their love expressed calorically.

Maybe loss and serious illness have not struck so close to your home. Still, there seems to be no break in the tide these days of baby announcements, PTO meal trains, and CaringBridge alerts for neighbors, friends, and relations. I'm utterly and indelibly convinced that providing a meal is the best way to show up for people. When you are unable to easily feed yourself, you get fed; when you are fluttering around unsure of how to be of use to others in need, you have an action plan. I also know that limited free time, the proliferation of restricted diets, and a lack of insider information (Are they vegetarians? Isn't she gluten-free? Is the middle child allergic to something?) can add up to paralyzing confusion about where to begin. Whether you want to send a meal to a family that has grown by one or to a neighbor who is grieving, it can be hard to know what to put together that will be welcome and hard to fit your caring gesture into your own busy life. It's useful to have some tricks up your sleeve for when the going gets rough, a kind of lexicon of support that you can (and should) tailor to the needs of your particular target but that gives you a place to start.

That's where this book comes in. It's intended as a guide to packing the baskets and boxes and trays that carry our love and concern from the heart of our homes to the tables and bellies of family and friends, neighbors and new faces. Organized by different life circumstances, you'll find more than seventy-five recipes to help you feed others, even strangers. It's a potent form of very practical magic, this sharing of food, and if we are going to cross the distances that divide us, this is solid footing to leap from.

Mother Teresa said, "There should be less talk. Take a broom and clean someone's house. That says enough." If you are moved to action when someone is in need, there is so much grace to be found in simple attention to the basics. More than training as a chef or encyclopedic knowledge of nutrition, having a rough sense of what may be required or desired in different situations is key. In each chapter you'll find recipes, but also strategies, ideas, and advice for approaching cooking for others in various circumstances. For example, someone struggling to find an appetite during chemo needs to be tempted, but her system is delicate and she may be acutely sensitive to certain smells or tastes; foods she loves could be off-limits, and eating may have become a chore. Pure, simple food that is presented beautifully is often the right move there. Someone struggling to remember to eat after a loss or other catastrophe also needs to be tempted, but pretty food is out of place when someone is overwhelmed by sadness. Don't leave room for the grieving person to wonder what he is eating, and make sure no explanations or instructions or special utensils are required. In both cases, there may be a small window of appetite to leap through, and it's good to make the leap count with maximal nutrition. A ravenous nursing mother, a depleted person rebuilding after a flu lays waste to the landscape, families putting down roots in a new home, students holed up for exams—everyone needs a meal, or at least a snack.

As you embark on a practice of feeding others, maintain open-mindedness—the crucial first layer of a philosophy of care. Encourage people to be honest with you about their likes and dislikes, what foods they may be craving, ones they may be avoiding, and even which of the things you made they responded to well. You can learn so much this way, especially if you approach it without ego and with a willingness to be creative inside the limits established by your recipient's tastes and beliefs. It's also important to keep your opinions on a short leash. Maybe you believe that something this person wants is bad for him, and maybe you believe something she professes to dislike is good for her. Maybe you think you have a lot of valuable data that would really serve the person well. Maybe you are just brimming with it. I encourage you to be very, very selective about sharing that kind of information. For the most part, and to generalize quite broadly, people are helped by what they perceive as helpful. Suggestions can of course be made. Knowledge can be shared. Minds can be changed. But times of stress are not usually the times when those things happen. If you believe brussels sprouts will cure her ailment, but brussels sprouts remind her of a terrible childhood incident involving a water gun, a mean babysitter, and six butterfly sutures, then keep the brussels sprouts out of the basket. She won't be served by them and neither will your connection to her. Showing up helpfully with food is a very close cousin to showing up quietly.

T his simple act of putting nourishment together in one home and taking it to another is one of the proudest accomplishments of civilization. Something tremendous happens when we care for each other in this way: our communities are strengthened by the filaments of compassion and assistance and shared experience that we weave from kitchen to table, from one home to another.

Everyone has to eat.

THE RECIPES, METHODS, AND INGREDIENTS

I like to satisfy the people I feed. Increasingly, those people have some limitation, some list of what they cannot, should not, or will not eat, and whether they are limited by morality, allergy, aversion, or illness, I still like to give them what they crave. I also have a magpie nature, in food terms. I like to grab flavors and ideas from all over the map. From those tendencies I have built a pantry, flavors I like and useful things I keep on hand, that informs the food you will find in these pages.

I've quelled the desire (it wasn't easy) to offer you five variations for each recipe, because the truth is that if my can't-eat-eggs sister wants lemon curd, I will try to make that happen in a way that tastes good. More than the variations, though, I want to commit space here to that idea. I'm not a big fan of faux food—tofu molded in the shape of a roast leg of lamb or vegan, gluten-free, paleo eclairs. But where there is a craving, there are ways to honor it, and I encourage you to find those in a manner that makes sense for the people you are feeding and for your personal tolerance for making an effort.

The baking recipes are the places this Dance of the Substitutions becomes most obvious in these pages. When I first started steering around wheat flour, for myself and other people I love who can't eat it, I freely confess I had about seventeen bags of weird flour at a time in the freezer. After some years at it, I'm now down to a handful of ride-or-dies (sweet rice, buckwheat, oat, tapioca, and coconut), my measure of their right to take up space in my pantry being how well they perform and how easily I can source them. If I've introduced a flour here, I've made sure it pops up a handful of times in the book, so you can see why it is worthwhile to have around and so you don't get saddled with half a bag of some oddment. Although I encourage you to try out the novel flours that appear in the book, I also include suggestions for using more familiar flours if that simplicity appeals to you. Note that anywhere regular all-purpose flour is called for, you can substitute a cup-for-cup style gluten-free blend. Recipes in the book were tested using King Arthur Gluten-Free Measure for Measure Flour. On that note, I cannot overstate the value of a kitchen scale for baking. I bake by weight. When converting between conventional and alternative flours, and really when baking in general, weight is a much more reliable predictor of success than volume.

Dairy is my dear companion, but that isn't true for everyone. When it comes to butter, pure coconut oil (the kind that is solid at room temperature) has a similar richness, and ghee (butter with the milk solids removed) is another often-well-tolerated alternative. I also use them because they taste good. Of the commercially available alternatives to cow's milk, I like coconut the best. Where coconut milk is suggested, I've indicated whether I mean the type that comes in a can or the one sold in a carton. The carton type of coconut milk is more or less interchangeable with dairy milk for most applications, and nut or soy milks are as well, if those are more appealing or suitable to your needs.

I like nuts for their nutrition and the rich flavor they bring to food, and use them frequently. Almonds are delicious! Cashews, too. They turn up in a lot of these recipes, as a result. But if the meal you are preparing isn't a good place for them, remember that sunflower seeds, pumpkin seeds, and the mighty hemp heart can often stand in. A need to boost iron intake for one of my children brought hemp hearts to my attention and I adore them; they're a nutritional powerhouse, are mild enough to win approval (or avoid trouble at least) just sprinkled on a salad, and they blend creamily into smoothies and dips with no need for presoaking. Five years ago, I'd never heard of them. Now, I always have a jar of them in my kitchen.

I live in a rural area, admittedly blessed with a couple fantastic grocery stores, but by no means a hub of commerce. Anything not quite ordinary that I've suggested you try here is something I either find locally or can easily order online. These two practices keep me in good shape between food-nerd excursions to bigger Asian, Indian, and Middle Eastern markets in more populous zip codes. My children can attest that I have low tolerance for most types of shopping, but pretty much endless capacity to wander a grocery store that caters to a culture not my own, looking for good deals on familiar items and new candidates for keeping on hand at all times.

At Indian markets, I look for bulk spices, rice, dried beans, hard-to-find fresh and frozen produce (okra!), and a variety of fresh chilies, plus snacks like frozen *pakora* and *pappadum* chips. At the Asian markets, I load up on noodles (so many gluten-free noodles!), exotic rices and other grains for Congee (page 104), dried peppers, seaweeds like *wakame* and *kombu*, and fresh miso paste. Rice flours are fresh and inexpensive, and the variety is impressive. I buy a lot of tea, interesting greens for stir-fries, tofu, and ginger in these spots, as well as all manner of amusing sweets and snacks to liven up care packages. Greek or Armenian markets offer a dizzying variety of feta cheeses, super-fresh bulk spices, giant jars of tomato paste, and exotic olives and jams to vary the lunch box fare.

While the recipes in this book may call for some new-to-you ingredients, the sentiment behind each dish calls on the familiar: the notion of care.

A Note on
PACKING AND
DELIVERING FOOD

Packing food successfully is not hard, but it definitely has a learning curve, so rest assured you are not the first person to have a dog step on the cake in the car. (Was that me? That was probably me.) Dogs aside, my first rule of meal-packing is to include a note in the box or basket describing the contents and offering instructions on assembling, reheating, or storing the meal. Also label each dish! Whether distracted by happiness, illness, sadness, or just life in general, people for the most part don't retain verbal instructions very well. Once you've delivered the box or basket and they are alone in the kitchen, it's nice if they can see specifics like "heat for 15 minutes at 350°" or "keep chilled" or "this is the dressing!" right on the thing. Because meal recipients may feel reluctant to express their dietary restrictions as thoroughly as they want or need to, including information about what is in the food spares a lot of awkwardness. And this seems like a good moment to assert that there is room on that piece of paper for other thoughts of celebration, encouragement, or condolence. I still have a few of the notes my family has received over the years with baskets of food, and not because of their reheating instructions.

The second rule, which is only second because you can't have two first rules, is that sturdy heatproof containers make all the difference for transporting food easily and safely from one house to another, and are a worthy step away from single-use plastics and their ilk. The third rule (another candidate for first rule) is that it's essential that you put your name on any containers you want back.

Here are some resources to consider when stocking your tool kit.

- KEEP A SHEET OF RETURN ADDRESS LABELS, A ROLL OF PAINTER'S TAPE, AND A PERMANENT MARKER HANDY TO COVER MOST LABELING NEEDS. ALL SHOULD WITHSTAND TRANSPORT AND WASHING. PERMANENT MARKER CAN BE WIPED OFF MOST SHINY SURFACES WITH ALCOHOL IF YOU NEED TO REMOVE IT.

- FOR VERSATILITY AND ECONOMY, IT'S HARD TO BEAT A MASON JAR. FROM THE TEENIEST JAM JARS TO THE HALF-GALLON KAHUNAS, THEY OFFER SECURE LIDS, THE HOLY GRAIL OF FOOD TRANSPORT. THE ECONOMICAL WAYS TO ACQUIRE THEM (BUYING IN BULK, FINDING AT YARD SALES, GETTING THEM FOR A SONG OR FOR FREE ON SITES LIKE CRAIGSLIST AND FREECYCLE) ALSO ALLOW FOR A PRETTY TRA-LA-LA ATTITUDE ABOUT HAVING THEM RETURNED TO YOU.

- YARD SALES ARE MORE THAN A GREAT PLACE TO FIND VINTAGE CANNING JARS: ALSO KEEP YOUR EYES OPEN FOR CASSEROLE DISHES AND OTHER CONTAINERS, SUCH AS CAKE-COVERS (I'M LOOKING AT YOU, DOG) AND CUPCAKE TOTES, TO BUILD YOUR PACK-IT-UP ARSENAL WITHOUT TAKING YOUR OWN HOUSEHOLD'S GO-TO DISHES OUT OF CIRCULATION FOR AS LONG AS IT TAKES YOU TO CIRCLE BACK AND PICK UP THE EMPTIES (WHICH SHOULD BE PROMPTLY, LET IT JUST BE SAID, UNLESS YOU HAVE ANNOUNCED THAT YOU DO NOT NEED THEM BACK AT ALL).

- MY BELOVED GLOBAL GROCERY STORES SELL A PLETHORA OF STORAGE CONTAINERS. CHINATOWN IS WHERE I SCORED MY FIRST GLASSLOCK VESSELS, AND STAINLESS STEEL TIFFIN CONTAINERS STOCKED IN INDIAN MARKETS ARE FANTASTIC FOR PICNICS AND LUNCH BOXES AND TRANSPORTING MEALS AND GARNISHES FROM HOUSE TO HOUSE.

- I HAVE A CABINET OF ATTRACTIVE TINS, BOXES, AND TUBES THAT OTHER THINGS CAME IN, WHICH I REPURPOSE WHEN PACKING THINGS FOR DELIVERY. TUCKING YOUR HOME-BAKED OFFERING INTO A HIGH-STYLE CONTAINER REALLY BRIGHTENS UP THE DELIVERY. I'M THINKING HERE OF THINGS AS FANCY AS THE GIFT TIN FROM SOME CLASSY TEA, AND AS UN-FANCY AS THE CARDBOARD SLIPCASE THAT SARDINE TINS ARE SOLD IN, WHICH IS JUST ABOUT THE SIZE OF A HOMEMADE BROWNIE, AND PROTECTS IT FROM DINGS IN TRANSPORT. THIS KIND OF DETAIL CAN ELEVATE YOUR PACKING FROM WELCOME SURPRISE TO TOTAL DELIGHT.

The tools are simple but well worth the time you take to consider them. Secure packing and clear information ensure that the fact that you have come to the door will be—as it should—the most memorable ingredient of your offering.

1

FOOD FOR EXPANDING FAMILIES

DID I SAY LOVE WAS LIKE
A BIG, DELICIOUS PIE?

OH, *PLEASE.*

I don't know what kind of
pie *you* like, but chances
are good that it doesn't
make you sit around cry-
ing into your Häagen–Dazs
and soaking through the
front of all your T-shirts
and yelling at everybody
at unpredictable intervals.

THAT'S THE KIND OF PIE
WE SEEM TO BE EATING AROUND HERE.

CATHERINE NEWMAN,
Waiting for Birdy

SINCE THE DAYS OF MY OWN CHILDREN'S BABYHOODS, I HAVE BEEN ON THE GIVING AND RECEIVING END OF DELIVERED MEALS FOR A HOST OF REASONS. THEY ARE ALL GOOD, SATISFYING WORK. BUT FOOD FOR FAMILIES THAT HAVE RECENTLY ACQUIRED BABIES REMAINS ONE OF MY FAVORITE MEALS TO COOK. I LOVE THINKING ABOUT WHEN MY CHILDREN WERE TINY AND SO I LOVE BEING AROUND NEW FAMILIES, WHERE THINGS FEEL NEST-Y AND POSSIBLE. ADAPTING TO THE NEEDS OF AN ENTIRELY DEPENDENT CREATURE IS A TOTALLY CONSUMING AND UTTERLY EXHAUSTING ENTERPRISE FOR THE NEW PARENTS, WHICH MAKES THE GIFT OF FOOD ALL THE MORE WELCOME. POSSIBLY MORE THAN ANY OTHER KIND OF RECIPIENT, NEW PARENTS LOVE LOVE LOVE THAT YOU HAVE BROUGHT THEM SOMETHING TO EAT, BECAUSE YOU HAVE REFUELED THEM AND REMINDED THEM THAT THERE IS A VILLAGE OUT THERE TO EMBRACE THEIR NEW PERSON.

My first child took her sweet time coasting down the birth canal, and the aftermath of her rather epic arrival happened to coincide with a closed-for-business hour in the hospital cafeteria. I hadn't eaten anything in over a day, and had devoted the bulk of the thirty hours since my last meal to a good amount of physical exertion. I was very, very, very hungry. Seeing the ravenous glint in my eye, the nurses rustled a droopy little sandwich that may have been egg salad and may have been chicken salad, or possibly tuna, from some hidden corner of the hospital. (A) I don't like any of those things. (B) It was repulsive. I inhaled it, and felt it rattle into the cavernous space of my hunger. All members of my immediate circle were down for the count, attempting to recoup a few of their own lost hours of sleep. Just as I began to think about eating the draperies, my middle sister appeared in the doorway of my hospital room to meet her niece, having made the two-and-a-half–hour drive from Boston in about ninety minutes with a hero sandwich (has any food ever been more aptly named?) from her favorite Italian market belted in on the passenger side. Fresh mozzarella, ricotta salata, roasted vegetables . . . I'm fairly certain I grunted while devouring it.

My sister stayed for a few days, and taught me more about heroism and the insightful ways to deploy it on a tray of food than I could have learned from any book. Drinks before I was thirsty, nourishing little nibbles before I knew I was hungry, a steady flow of hearty mama-bear fare to sustain my sleep-deprived and recovering body. I enjoyed her attentions immensely, but I don't think I fully appreciated them until she left, and I found myself slamming into walls of hunger with none of her intuitive first aid to come to my rescue. I started keeping whole roasted yams everywhere—diaper bag, bedside, car—as a kind of emergency ration/oxygen mask. Because I generally stink at asking for help and frankly didn't even consider that it might be available, we stumbled through most of that daughter's infancy eating what I could throw together quickly with one eye open and one arm free.

As we approached the launch date of the second baby (whom I planned to birth at home, partially so I could be closer to the fridge), a newish friend asked me an odd question: "Who's doing your food?" From time to time, when chatting with another person in one's native tongue, one can encounter a sentence made up of words that are entirely recognizable while its meaning remains elusive. This was just such a time. When she perceived the mental echo on my part that her question had set off, she rephrased it. "Your meals, I mean. Who is in charge of your meals?" These, too, were all words I knew well, but I still couldn't make out the gist of the question. Though by this time my little family had left the solitary moon of Pluto on which first-time parents sometimes find themselves, and had a nice little network of other young families around us, we had yet to see in action one of the best reasons I know of to make friends.

Eventually, using a combination of patience and semaphore and monosyllables comprehensible even to my gestational brain, this friend introduced me to the concept of the meal train. *Baby: The Sequel* opened the door to a whole new world. Kind Feeding Friend set up a schedule among our nursery-school parent group, with the result that every few days, hot food came to the door right at the hour when how much we needed it was colliding with our utter inability to provide it for ourselves. It was heaven. From that day forward, I pledged myself to this gorgeous system of interfamilial feeding.

A note of advice when offering food to new-baby households: Meal delivery time is always a good time to flex the muscles of self-restraint that, when relaxed, lead a person to opine freely. The conversational path is littered with temptations to talk about how your own stitches healed, how breastfeeding unfolded for your sister-in-law who had the *identical shape nipples,* how the attachment process went for your neighbor's cousin who also just adopted from the same country, how the amount of sleeping or burping or housecleaning or hair-brushing you experienced personally compares to what you are observing or hearing about in this household. Don't. Give. In. Even if the new parents appear to be actively seeking information, be really thoughtful about what you offer. What they seem to be asking probably masks what they are really, truly asking.

I worked as a peer-counselor for new families for about fifteen years. I saw people who were legitimately flattened by becoming responsible for an infant whose photo and biography could have illustrated the Wiki for "Easy as Pie"; I also saw parents who calmly rose to a list of challenges and trials in their infant's early days that suggested they had lost a bet with a malevolent spirit. Across all situations—the ones solved in a single five-minute phone call and the ones that required hours of talk and visit time to make better, let alone fix—parents were basically asking this: "Will we be okay?" And its corollary, "When will we feel like we know what to do?" However straightforward (or not) their stories, all parents are scaling mountains. With the possible exception of the couple in our first birth preparation course who produced a ten-pound infant after three hours of uncomplicated labor and reported that birth was "kind of anticlimactic, after all those classes," the transition from relative autonomy to parenthood is among the most significant that we face in life, with a huge *you alone hold the bag here* overlay that few other events can match.

What "okay" looks like for each family will vary hugely. What feels like a huge victory will, too. One person's first solo trip to the grocery store, after which everyone including the cashier needs a bath and a nap, is another person's five hours in the surgical NICU waiting room. These things do not compare, in the sense that comparison is absolutely antithetical to building community, which is what that dinner basket is all about. If you are a parent yourself, you can probably recall the way it felt to be utterly overwhelmed when a tiny human was first deemed to be your responsibility, and you can probably also summon the memory of a moment that came later (maybe much later) when you *finally* understood that a particular cry meant a wet diaper or you achieved some other similar miracle of cross-cultural understanding with the small alien being now in charge of your days and nights. Tap into that well of compassion before bestowing your opinion on any new parent, because whatever the age of your children, I bet a whole hot dinner you can also remember, still, the sting of someone's offhand, even possibly well-intended, comment about your precious offspring and/or your coping strategies (a.k.a., parenting) at a time when you were least equipped to be flexible in your interpretations.

Because those are grateful eaters, those people who answer the doorbell where a new person is, it's hard to miss with that basket of food. Still, extra value points are added if it is healthy, substantial, and appealing to all the ranking adults as well as any emotionally stricken toddlers in residence. And five gold stars if the food is on a stick, because even children who aren't adjusting to a new sibling like food on a stick, as do parents grabbing food with one hand as they blow by the kitchen en route to the changing table or the washing machine. Food that can be eaten at its arrival temperature, or responds calmly to being chilled now and heated up later, or tastes fine eaten standing in front of the fridge in the middle of the night, is a major win here. You don't need to have a new baby to look favorably on a meal like that, of course, but being near one really ups the appreciation factor.

Those fifteen years as a counselor to nursing mothers, and also as a parent to a fussy eater, mean that anything that is spicy or associated with disrupted digestion (mainly alliums and brassicas) sit this round out in my kitchen. I like the challenge of making things that are flavorful and satisfying without those to rely on. You can, of course, put the members of these families back in, if such considerations are not relevant.

My favorite kind of new-baby meal is modular, with many ways to customize it to individual tastes. I trace the roots of this idea to when my oldest child was about three years old, and the parents at her preschool decided to produce a cookbook. One of the best sections of the book is a compendium of little ways to get reluctant eaters to eat. This is where I learned to employ the kebab trick, and also learned the power of dip and other ways to make a meal into a low-key build-a-bear workshop. If the family you are making a meal for includes an older brother or sister aged somewhere between toddler and tween, there's a good chance that that person, whose life has already been disrupted by baby business, is in no mood for scraping off sauces or hunting among the mushrooms to find something palatable on the plate. The recipes that follow include three complete meals, with options for meat-eaters and vegetarians, that follow the rough formula of a super-flavorful protein, a carbohydrate, a vegetable, and a sauce that can unite them all or just keep to itself.

A MEXICAN-INSPIRED MEAL

There is something undeniably satisfying about hearty Mexican flavors, some quality that endures even without the fiery heat that often distinguishes this cuisine. This dinner, in either its omnivore or vegetarian versions, is especially conducive (thanks, corn tortillas!) to eating with whichever hand is free of babies and tots.

CARNITAS

Carnitas are crazy simple, easily doubled, and always devoured. You can substitute boiled new potatoes for the roasted yams here; in that case, I like to smash them while they are hot, and toss them with the pork.

SERVES 4 TO 6

For the
PORK

3 pounds boneless pork
   shoulder or butt
1 bay leaf
1 teaspoon kosher salt
½ cup orange juice
½ teaspoon finely grated
   orange zest
2 teaspoons ground cumin
½ teaspoon smoked
   paprika

½ teaspoon crushed
   dried oregano

For the
ROASTED SWEET
POTATOES

2 medium sweet
   potatoes or yams
   (about 1½ pounds),
   cut into 2-inch cubes
2–3 teaspoons olive oil

To
SERVE

Corn tortillas, warm
Wedges of lime
Bright Simple Salad
   (page 23), or some
   cubes of avocado and
   chopped cilantro

1   Trim any especially thick fat from the surface of the pork and discard. Cut the meat into 1- to 2-inch cubes, discarding any that are pure fat. Put the pork, bay leaf, salt, orange juice, and zest in a large pot. Add enough water to cover the meat by 2–3 inches.

2   Bring the mixture barely to a boil, then immediately reduce the heat to sustain a simmer. Other than periodically skimming off and discarding any foam that forms on the surface, this is a pretty hands-off stage. Simmer uncovered for 1½ hours, until the pork is very soft;

recipe continues

if your meat is not tender by the time most of the water has cooked off, add water to keep the meat submerged until a cube comes easily apart when pressed with the tines of a fork.

3 While the pork is cooking, preheat the oven to 375°F. Toss the sweet potato cubes with the oil and spread them on a parchment-lined baking sheet. Roast them for 20–30 minutes, tossing once or twice during that time, until tender and lightly browned.

4 Remove the bay leaf from the pot, raise the heat to medium, and cook off the remaining liquid, stirring frequently until it is gone. Add the cumin, paprika, and oregano, and continue to cook for another 5–7 minutes, until the meat begins to crisp in the rendered fat, scraping the pan often to reincorporate the crisped bits. Once it is crisped to your liking, let it stand off the heat for 5 minutes; this rest will help loosen the last stuck bits so you can remove it all to your serving (or transport) container. Allow to cool before covering.

5 You can encourage diners to make their own soft tacos by taking a warmed tortilla, loading it to their liking with carnitas, potatoes, and salad, and topping it off with a squeeze of lime, or you can toss the potatoes with the meat, and serve with the tortillas and other bits on the side.

TOFU CHORIZO

This recipe was inspired by a Mark Bittman recipe in the New York Times. *If you are familiar with tofu and always looking for new ways to use it, it's a great addition to the repertoire; it's been in frequent rotation since I discovered it. If you are scared of tofu or can't imagine how it could possibly taste like anything, this is the place to start. It's super flavorful and makes a welcome surprise in a meal train, where it's unlikely to be a repeat of anything that came before it.*

SERVES 4 TO 6

3 tablespoons olive oil, divided

1 medium carrot, finely chopped

Two 15-ounce blocks firm tofu

1 tablespoon ancho chili powder

2 teaspoons ground cumin

⅛ teaspoon ground cinnamon

2 teaspoons cider vinegar

Salt and freshly ground pepper

½ cup finely chopped fresh cilantro

For the
ROASTED SWEET POTATOES

2 medium sweet potatoes or yams

(about 1½ pounds), cut into 2-inch cubes

2–3 teaspoons olive oil

To
SERVE

Corn tortillas, wedges of lime, warm

Bright Simple Salad (page 23), or some cubes of avocado and chopped cilantro

1 Put 2 tablespoons of the oil in a large heavy skillet set over medium heat. Sauté the carrot for about 5 minutes, until it softens and begins to brown.

recipe continues

2 With your hands, crumble the tofu into the pan; just squeeze it like the Hulk, letting some inch-size pieces and some smaller pieces extrude from your mighty fists.

3 Increase the heat to medium-high and cook, stirring occasionally, until the obvious moisture in the tofu has cooked off, about 5–7 minutes.

4 Add the remaining 1 tablespoon oil and continue to cook, scraping the bottom of the skillet and adjusting the heat as necessary, until the tofu browns and crisps to your liking. This can take up to 30 minutes. It will go slowly at first, as the remaining moisture cooks out, and then begin to pick up speed; you'll need to stir and scrape more and more frequently toward the end of the cooking time.

5 While the tofu is cooking, preheat the oven to 375°F. Toss the sweet potato cubes with the oil and spread them on a parchment-lined baking sheet. Roast them, tossing once or twice, for 20–30 minutes, until tender and lightly browned.

6 Sprinkle the tofu with the chili powder, cumin, and cinnamon; stir and cook, continuing to scrape any browned bits from the bottom of the pan until the mixture is fragrant, another 1 or 2 minutes. If you have a lot of stuck bits, add 1 or 2 tablespoons of water to help to loosen them. Stir in the vinegar and use the salt and pepper to adjust the seasoning to your taste. Stir in the cilantro.

7 Encourage diners to make their own soft tacos by taking a warmed tortilla, loading it with the tofu, sweet potato, and salad, and topping it off with a squeeze of lime. Or toss the potatoes with the tofu and cilantro, and serve with the tortillas and other bits on the side.

BRIGHT SIMPLE SALAD

This salad gets a lot of its merit from the way it is composed. Sent as prepped components with a separate container of dressing, it allows small people who don't like one food to touch another food to choose exactly what they want before it turns into a mixed salad for the grown-ups. It also gains points for being tart and sweet and salty all at once, and for coming together with just a few minutes of casual chopping.

SERVES 4 TO 6

1 firm-ripe mango, peeled and cut into ½-inch cubes

Flesh of 2 firm-ripe avocados, cut into ½-inch cubes

1 English (or 3 or 4 Persian) cucumbers, quartered lengthwise and thickly sliced

½ cup fresh cilantro leaves, coarsely chopped

1 large handful fresh sunflower sprouts, coarsely chopped

2 tablespoons hemp hearts, pepitas, or sunflower seeds

For the
DRESSING

½ teaspoon ground cumin

½ teaspoon Maldon or kosher salt

1 tablespoon lime juice

2 tablespoons extra-virgin olive oil

1 It's best to toss everything together right before serving. If I'm preparing it ahead, I toss the avocado with a squeeze of lime juice to keep it bright before layering all the vegetables in their travel container. I send the dressing and seeds in separate little jars.

AN EASTERN-INSPIRED MEAL

I spent some time traveling in Thailand and was captivated by the omnipresence of micro-restaurants—someone with a wok, grill, and cashbox seemed to be on every corner. When I'm ravenous, I gravitate to those flavors: salty and smoky and citrusy.

SUPER SAVORY GROUND KEBABS

with
UNPEANUT SAUCE

These kebabs are easily made as little burgers if you don't want to mess around with skewers, but stick or no stick, make them oblong to facilitate dipping. The fragrant rice powder is a great secret weapon as a thickener and binder, bringing a lot of flavor to the task. If tender bellies are not a consideration, a little fire is a nice addition to these; you might send some Sriracha on the side for anyone who can take the heat. If you can't find the lime leaves, the finely grated zest of one lime or a teaspoon of very finely minced fresh lemongrass are equally delicious substitutes.

SERVES 4 TO 6

12 small bamboo or
   metal skewers
1 tablespoon basmati
   or other long-grain
   white rice
2–3 fresh makrut lime
   leaves, center rib torn
   out
1 pound ground meat
   (turkey, pork, beef, or
   chicken)

2 tablespoons fish
   sauce
1 tablespoon grated
   fresh ginger
1 tablespoon coconut
   sugar or brown sugar
¼ cup finely minced
   fresh basil
¼ cup finely minced
   fresh mint

¼ cup finely minced
   fresh cilantro

To
SERVE
UnPeanut Sauce
   (recipe follows)

1 If you are using bamboo skewers, submerge them in a dish of water to soak.

recipe continues

2   In a small heavy sauté pan, heat the rice, dry, for about 2 minutes, until lightly toasted and fragrant, stirring or shaking the pan frequently. Remove from the heat and toss the lime leaves in with the hot rice, stirring once or twice, and then dump the contents of the pan into a spice grinder or blender. Grind to a fine powder.

3   Combine the rice powder in a medium bowl with the meat, fish sauce, ginger, sugar, basil, mint, and cilantro, and stir thoroughly (it's easiest to use your hands). Refrigerate for 30 minutes to allow the rice powder to hydrate.

4   Using dampened hands, form a sausage of about 2 tablespoons of the meat mixture around each of the skewers, and set them into the fridge again while you heat the grill, grill pan, or broiler. Cook for 6–8 minutes on each side, until lightly charred and cooked through. Cool to room temperature before wrapping loosely in foil or packing into an oven-safe covered dish. Serve with UnPeanut Sauce.

UNPEANUT SAUCE

Rich in nutrients and health benefits and general yumminess, cashews step in for peanuts here to make a gentler, creamier version of the usual satay sauce.

MAKES ABOUT 1½ CUPS

1 cup dry-roasted, unsalted cashews

2 teaspoons finely grated fresh ginger

½ teaspoon finely grated orange zest

1 tablespoon toasted sesame oil

2 teaspoons coconut sugar or brown sugar

1 tablespoon tamari or soy sauce

2 tablespoons lime juice

1 tablespoon orange juice

⅓ cup light canned coconut milk

1   Soak the cashews in water to cover for at least 1 hour or up to overnight.

2   Drain the cashews and place in a blender. Add the ginger, zest, oil, sugar, tamari, lime juice, orange juice, and coconut milk, and blend until quite smooth.

3   Transfer to a mason jar or other lidded container, and store in the refrigerator for up to a week.

TOFU SATAY

with
UNPEANUT SAUCE

A similarly zippy flavor profile to the one that makes the meat version sing takes aim at tofu here, waking it up from its usual stir-fry slumber with a soak in a hotrod coconut marinade.

SERVES 4 TO 6

12 small bamboo or metal skewers

Two 15-ounce blocks firm or extra-firm tofu

For the
MARINADE

2 teaspoons finely grated fresh ginger

1 tablespoon finely minced lemongrass, tender inner bulb only

1 teaspoon cumin seeds, toasted and ground, or 1¼ teaspoons ground cumin

1 teaspoon coriander seeds, toasted and lightly crushed, or 1¼ teaspoons ground coriander

1 teaspoon ground turmeric

1 tablespoon tamari or soy sauce

1 tablespoon lime juice

1 tablespoon coconut sugar or brown sugar

½ cup light canned coconut milk

To
SERVE

UnPeanut Sauce (page 27)

1   If you are using bamboo skewers, submerge them in a dish of water to soak for at least 1 hour before using.

2   Cut each tofu block in half horizontally to create two thinner slices. Arrange the four pieces on a wad of paper towels or clean cotton kitchen towels, folding the towels over the top of the tofu as well; place a plate or cutting board on top, along with a large can or heavy book to weigh it down further. Leave this arrangement for 20–30 minutes, so most of the water is pressed from the tofu.

3   Make the marinade. Whisk together the ginger, lemongrass, cumin seeds, coriander seeds, turmeric, tamari, lime juice, sugar, and coconut milk in a medium bowl.

4   Cut each tofu slice into eight cubes and drop them in the marinade, tossing gently to coat. Cover tightly and chill for at least 1 hour or up to overnight.

5   Thread the cubes onto the skewers while you preheat a grill, grill pan, or broiler, and lightly oil the surface of the pan before cooking the skewers for 5–7 minutes per side, turning to ensure even browning. Cool to room temperature before wrapping loosely in foil or packing into an oven-safe covered dish. Serve with UnPeanut Sauce.

NOODLES WITH OPTIONS

If you are preparing a meal basket for a household with a little resident fussbudget, keep the noodles, vegetables, and dressing in separate containers for transport. Then the taxed toddler who simply cannot take one other thing can have his plain noodles and his parents can have a satisfying dinner and peace for ten minutes. If it's a no-holds-barred situation, toss the noodles and vegetables together, but still send the dressing along separately; it's best to dress this cold noodle dish just a few minutes before eating.

SERVES 4 TO 6

For the
DRESSING

2 tablespoons toasted sesame oil

2 tablespoons tamari or soy sauce

2 teaspoons honey or maple syrup

1 tablespoon brown rice vinegar

Zest and juice of 1 lime

1 tablespoon finely grated fresh ginger

½ cup chopped fresh cilantro

½ cup chopped fresh mint

½ cup chopped fresh basil

For the
NOODLES

One 8-ounce package black rice noodles or any soba-style noodle

1 teaspoon neutral vegetable oil

4–6 handfuls (about 5 ounces) baby spinach

1 English cucumber (about 10 ounces)

1 Put the sesame oil, tamari, honey, vinegar, lime zest and juice, ginger, cilantro, mint, and basil in a small jar with a secure lid and shake well. Taste and adjust sweet, tart, and salty to your preferences.

2   Bring a large pot of salted water to a brisk boil and cook the noodles about 7 minutes, until tender, stirring often to prevent sticking. Drain and rinse the cooked noodles with cool water; this stops the cooking and gets rid of excess starch. While the noodles are still pretty wet from rinsing, toss them with the oil; this prevents clumping.

3   Wash and dry the spinach thoroughly (grit is very disappointing). Remove any bits of tough stem and any of the skeevy leaves that always seem to hide among the bright ones. Use a super-sharp knife to slice the leaves into thin ribbons.

4   Remove the ends from the cucumber and cut it into 4-inch logs. Slice each log lengthwise into ¼-inch slices, then cut again at a 90-degree angle to the first cut to make ¼-inch matchsticks. Toss the cucumber matchsticks and spinach ribbons together.

5   Pack the noodles into one bowl and the vegetables into a second, and send the dressing along in its little jar.

A MEDITERRANEAN–
INSPIRED MEAL

Meal train recipients tend to experience a lot of chicken and tofu. It's a challenge to steer these proteins through novel enough territory that their welcome does not get worn out. This bowl is fueled by standard grocery fare that is reliable year-round and swings well outside the teriyaki zone as it delivers nourishment.

CITRUSY GRILLED CHICKEN OR TOFU SKEWERS

with
ROASTED CARROT ROMESCO

Sweet orange, tart lime, and tangy yogurt tenderize the chicken, flavor-ize the tofu, and balance out the bright herbs. All together, maybe they could make an exhausted new parent think just for a second that the family is on a patio overlooking the sea, with clean shirts on the humans, a clean tablecloth on the table, and the surf gently washing the rocks on the beach. There's some marinating time in the instructions here, so make sure your plan of attack allows for that.

SERVES 4 TO 6

8 bamboo or metal
   skewers
2 pounds boneless
   chicken (breasts,
   tenders, or thighs), or
   two 15-ounce blocks
   firm or extra-firm tofu
1 lemon
½ orange
2 dozen pitted green
   olives

Vegetable oil, for
   greasing the grill

For the
MARINADE
1 cup plain whole milk
   Greek yogurt
2 tablespoons olive oil
2 teaspoons sweet
   paprika
2 tablespoons minced
   fresh basil

2 teaspoons minced
   fresh thyme
Zest of 1 lemon
2 tablespoons lemon
   juice
1 teaspoon orange zest
1 tablespoon orange
   juice
1 teaspoon salt
½ teaspoon freshly
   ground pepper

1   If you are using bamboo skewers, submerge them in a dish of water to soak for at least 1 hour before using.

recipe continues

2   Trim the chicken and cut it into large bite-size pieces. For tofu, cut each block in half horizontally to create two thinner slices. Arrange the four pieces on a wad of paper towels or clean cotton kitchen towels, folding the towels over the top of the tofu as well; place a plate or cutting board on top, along with a large can or heavy book to weigh it down further. Leave this arrangement for 20–30 minutes, so most of the water is pressed from the tofu.

3   Make the marinade. Combine the yogurt, olive oil, paprika, basil, thyme, lemon zest, lemon juice, orange zest, orange juice, salt, and pepper in a medium bowl.

4   Cut the whole lemon and half an orange for the skewers into quarters, lengthwise, and slice the quarters crossways into ½-inch slices. Flick out any obvious seeds.

5   Thread the chicken or the drained, cubed tofu onto the skewers, folding the chicken as needed for pieces that are long and thin, alternating with slices of lemon, orange, and olives. Load the kebabs in a baking dish, and spoon or brush the marinade all over them, coating well. Cover and refrigerate at least 4 hours or up to overnight.

6   Preheat a grill or grill pan at medium-high heat or your broiler. Grill the skewers until golden brown and cooked through, turning skewers occasionally, 10–15 minutes. Cool to room temperature before wrapping loosely in foil or packing into an oven-safe covered dish.

ROASTED CARROT ROMESCO

Carrots step in for the usual roasted peppers here, bringing their orange-vegetable benefits to a silky, nourishing, and flavorful accent for any roasted or grilled meat. This also works as a dip or spread for raw and cooked vegetables.

MAKES ABOUT 1½ CUPS

¼ cup hemp hearts, slivered almonds, or sunflower seeds

1½ pounds carrots, peeled and cut into 1-inch chunks

¼ cup extra-virgin olive oil, divided

1 teaspoon honey or agave syrup

¼ teaspoon coriander seeds

¼ cup coarsely chopped flat-leaf parsley leaves (stems removed)

Juice of 1–2 lemons (about 3 tablespoons)

1 teaspoon smoked paprika

½ teaspoon salt

½ cup water

1   If you are using almonds or sunflower seeds, soak them in a small bowl with water to cover while you prepare the other ingredients. This yields a creamier result. Hemp hearts do not require soaking.

2   Preheat the oven to 375°F, and line a baking sheet with parchment paper.

3   Toss the carrots with 2 tablespoons of the olive oil, the honey, and the coriander seeds. Spread the seasoned carrots on the prepared baking sheet and roast for 20–25 minutes, until tender and lightly caramelized in spots, tossing a few times as they cook.

recipe continues

4   Remove the carrots to a blender or food processor. Add the remaining 2 tablespoons olive oil, parsley, lemon juice, paprika, salt, water, and hemp hearts (or drained almonds or sunflower seeds). Pulse to combine, then continue pulsing until a coarse puree forms. You may need to add additional water, one tablespoon at a time, to get things moving. Taste and add additional salt and/or lemon to balance the flavors to your liking.

5   Scrape the sauce into a jar or other container with a secure lid. The sauce will keep refrigerated for a week.

ZUCCHINI ME-MO

My sister invented this side dish that is heaven with fresh, waxy, gorgeous summer zucchini from the farmer's market or garden, and is also a fine way to perk up more fatigued winter grocery store zucchini. It is shockingly delicious for something so simple and plain. I made it for a friend once and some weeks later she asked for the recipe.

"You use that slicer side of your box grater," I explained, "the side no one ever uses, and then you just cook it superfast in a whole lot of very hot oil."

"Hmm," said the friend, "isn't that frying, that action you are describing?" She had a point, but I have to say this is so not fried in flavor and feel that I am going to hold true to my original description.

It's essential that you don't add salt here, because salt makes zucchini weep and water inhibits the fr–, ah, very fast cooking in oil. I really don't think you will miss it.

SERVES 4 TO 6

Four 7-inch zucchini	¼ cup excellent extra-virgin olive oil, divided	Zest of ½ lemon Freshly ground pepper

1 Wash the zucchini and trim the blossom ends off, leaving the stems to use as handles. Using the slicing side of a box grater, slice the zucchini thinly and unevenly, so that some pieces have a paper-thin edge on one side. I like to keep rotating the squash a quarter turn as I go. This is easier to do than it is to describe, and is over with so fast and accomplished so well by the box grater that involving a food processor or mandoline is more bother than help.

recipe continues

2   Heat 2 tablespoons of the oil in a heavy skillet over medium-high heat. When the oil is rippling, add half the shaved squash. Dividing into two batches ensures no pan crowding and consequently no steaming; the squash slices should basically be in a single layer. Let it cook undisturbed for 2–3 minutes, so that some of the squash gets browned and almost sticks, then scrape and toss until it is all bright in color and browned bits are evident throughout, about another minute. Remove to a serving dish. Repeat with the remaining squash and the remaining 2 tablespoons oil. Season with the zest and a twist of pepper.

3   This waits comfortably at room temperature until serving time, and though it can stand a quick reheating, uncovered, in a pan or oven, I find it really is tastiest at room temperature.

GREEN RICE

Green rice is better than plain rice because it has all kinds of nutritional oomph from its stealthy and not-so-stealthy (it is green, after all) ingredients. You can tell any older siblings who may be in the house that it comes from Mars.

SERVES 4 TO 6

2 cups sweet brown or short-grain brown rice

1½ teaspoons salt, divided

4¼ cups water, divided

4 handfuls (about 3 ounces) baby spinach leaves

2 tablespoons unsalted butter, melted

1 teaspoon nutritional yeast

½ teaspoon mild curry powder

1 Combine the rice, ½ teaspoon of the salt, and 4 cups of the water in a medium saucepan and bring to a full boil. Turn the heat down to low and nearly cover the pot. Simmer for about 30 minutes, until almost all the water is absorbed, fitting the cover snugly once the danger of eruption is past.

2 Stir the rice and cover, turning off the heat. Let it rest and steam for 10 minutes.

3 Combine the spinach and the remaining ¼ cup water in a blender and completely blitz the greens until you have emerald-green juice. Whisk this juice, the remaining 1 teaspoon salt, nutritional yeast, and curry powder with the melted butter, and dump this over the hot rice, combining the two completely. This can be held at room temperature for up to 4 hours, or refrigerated for later consumption. It should be heated, covered in foil, in a warm oven (250–300°F) just until heated through.

SUNSET TO SUNRISE OATS

Overnight oats are kind of a Thing, but unlike some Things, there's a good basis to their fame. A few minutes of mixing on the evening of day one gives you breakfast without a moment's work on day two and for many days to come. The dead-simple method can lead to all kinds of madness as different milks, fruits, and flavors get in on the party. In this case, all the colors of the glorious sunrise—the same one that the wee babe is waking her parents up to see—manifest in a bowl of powerful nutrition. And if there was this one time you subbed cocoa powder for the Golden Milk Mix, well—babies can't tweet. No one ever needs to know breakfast was chocolate.

SERVES 4 TO 6

2 teaspoons Golden Milk Mix (pages 202)

2 tablespoons honey

2 tablespoons very hot water

1 cup cow's milk, carton-type coconut milk, or almond milk (or a mixture)

½ cup plain whole-milk yogurt

¼ teaspoon sea salt

½ teaspoon vanilla extract

⅔ cup old-fashioned rolled oats

2 tablespoons golden flax meal or chia seeds, or a combination

2 tablespoons hemp hearts

2 tablespoons crushed freeze-dried strawberries

2 tablespoons finely shredded raw carrot

1 tablespoon minced crystallized ginger

1   Combine the Golden Milk Mix, honey, and hot water in a medium-sized mixing bowl, stirring well to dissolve the honey. Stir in the milk, yogurt, salt, and vanilla.

2 Add the oats, flax/chia, and hemp hearts to the bowl, stirring well to combine, then swirl in the berries, carrots, and ginger.

3 Divide the mixture among four to six individual jelly jars.

4 Cap tightly and chill overnight (minimum) or up to 3 days.

OTHER WAYS TO DO IT

- FRESH BERRIES OR OTHER SLICED, FRESH FRUIT REALLY PERK UP THESE JARS.

- CREATE A PARFAIT EFFECT BY LAYERING COOKED FRUIT OR JAM WITH THE OATS AS YOU BUILD THE JARS.

- YOU CAN REPLACE THE YOGURT WITH AN EQUIVALENT AMOUNT OF MILK; JUST DOUBLE THE FLAX OR CHIA TO THICKEN THINGS UP.

CINNAMON APPLE MUFFINS

These muffins are an excellent way to start the day, with loads of protein from the almonds and the goodness of cinnamon making the house smell like all will be well. They are adapted from a recipe by Comfy Belly's Erica Kerwien, who is a great resource for making treats using a limited list of ingredients. Nothing about these gluten-free muffins tastes of restriction; these taste more like cinnamon buns, but without the post-consumption nap those often require.

MAKES 10 MUFFINS

1½ cups peeled, chopped apple chunks, roughly 1- to 2-inches

1½ teaspoons ground cinnamon

½ cup + 2 tablespoons plain whole-milk yogurt or a dairy-free substitute

⅓ cup honey or maple syrup

2 eggs

1 teaspoon vanilla extract

2½ cups (240g) almond flour

1 cup (128g) oat bran

2 tablespoons tapioca flour or cornstarch

½ teaspoon sea salt

½ teaspoon baking soda

½ teaspoon baking powder

For the
TOPPING

1 tablespoon ground cinnamon

¼ cup honey

3 tablespoons unsalted butter, softened, ghee, or coconut butter

¼ teaspoon sea salt

1 Preheat the oven to 325° F. Spray or butter a twelve-cup muffin pan.

2 Toss the apple chunks with the cinnamon in a medium bowl.

3 In a separate medium bowl, combine the yogurt, honey, eggs, and vanilla, and blend well with a wooden spoon.

4 Put the almond flour, oat bran, tapioca flour, salt, baking soda, and baking powder in a small bowl and mix until well combined.

5 Add the dry ingredients to the wet ingredients and stir until combined. Put 2 tablespoons of batter in each cup, reserving the remainder.

6 Make the topping. In a small bowl, cream together the cinnamon, honey, butter, and salt.

7 Separate the topping into two-thirds and one-third (I usually just very scientifically draw a line in the bowl, a little to one side of what seems like the middle) and divide the larger portion among the filled muffin cups (about a teaspoon per cup), plopping it into each center.

8 Distribute the seasoned apples, five or six pieces per cup, pressing them lightly into the batter and topping. Then divide the remaining batter among the cups, dropping it on top of the apples, which it may not cover completely.

9 Evenly distribute the remaining topping over the top of each muffin. Bake for about 25 minutes, until a toothpick placed in the center of a muffin comes out clean and the edges are starting to brown.

SUN SALUTATIONS COOKIES

You know those recipes that gallop all over the Internet, the ones for ice cream or cupcakes or fudge made from only three ingredients? Mostly ignore those. Waffle nachos, for example? A bust, trust me (and please help me clean my waffle iron). That said, it pays to occasionally be taken in by a trend, and that idea about the three-item peanut butter cookies had some merit. This version ups the ingredient count, but it also skips over the maligned and combative peanut, substituting richly nutritious sunflower seed butter for a please-all, flourless cookie that lives in the place between gingersnaps and things that are good for you. Sunflower seed butter is softer than its peanut cousin, so flaxseed meal joins up to hold things together and deliver its high-powered nutrition to boot. Add the optional filling, and suddenly the Nutter Butter of your youth is all grown up, ready to nourish and entertain some hungry new parents.

MAKES ABOUT 36 COOKIES OR 18 SANDWICH COOKIES

1 cup sunflower seed butter

1 cup coconut sugar

1 egg

3 tablespoons flax meal

2 teaspoons grated fresh ginger, or 1 teaspoon ground ginger

Pinch of sea salt

For the
FILLING
(OPTIONAL)

¼ cup vegetable shortening (I like Spectrum)

¼ cup sunflower seed butter

½ cup well-sifted confectioner's sugar

1 teaspoon heavy cream, coconut cream, or non-dairy creamer

¾ teaspoon Maldon or other flaky salt

1 Combine the sunflower seed butter, sugar, egg, flax meal, ginger, and salt in a medium bowl and stir well. Refrigerate the mixture for at least 30 minutes for ease of handling.

2   Preheat the oven to 350°F, and line two baking sheets with parchment paper.

3   Using your hands, roll nickel-size globs of dough into smooth balls and place them 2 inches apart on the lined baking sheets.

4   Flatten each ball to ¼-inch thinness with a flat-bottom drinking glass.

5   Bake for 8–10 minutes, reversing the sheets for even baking at the midpoint of that time, until edges are coloring and tops are set. Take care not to overbake; these burn faster than you might think. Allow to set for 5 minutes on the sheet, then use a thin spatula to remove to a rack to finish cooling.

6   For the filling, if using, cream the shortening in a small bowl, then beat in the sunflower seed butter, followed by the sugar. Add the cream and mix it in completely, then stir in the flaky salt. It should be spreadable but not runny, a true frosting consistency, so add a drop more cream if it is too thick.

7   Use a generous teaspoon or two of filling for each sandwich, dropping it into the center of one cookie and pressing the second cookie on top to spread the filling to the edges.

2

FOOD
FOR THE
REARRANGED
AND
RELOCATED

GETTING FOOD DELIVERED
TO MY HOME
COMBINES TWO OF
MY FAVORITE ACTIVITIES:
EATING
AND NOT MOVING.

JIM GAFFIGAN,
Food: A Love Story

WE DO OUR BEST TO MASK AND MITIGATE IT, BUT EVEN THE MOST FREE-FLOATING SPIRITS AMONG US ARE, IF NOT CREATURES OF HABIT, CREATURES AT LEAST. WE ORIENT OUR ANIMAL SELVES AROUND FEEDING AND SLEEPING, AND EVEN PEOPLE WHO THRIVE ON VARIETY CAN FIND THAT WHEN THE BASIC CREATURE COMFORTS ARE TOO MUCH OF AN OPEN QUESTION, FRAZZLING AND DISCOMBOBULATION SOON FOLLOW.

H ave you ever been taken in by the apparent convenience of an overnight flight? In principle, the logistics of leaving your departure city in the evening and arriving at your destination in the morning sound just right for the rhythm of human life—you board, you dine, you sleep, you wake up, you land—but in practice, the net result is more like having all the bolts loosened on your sense of time and place and other crucial aspects of orientation. I tend to get not one wink on a plane, getting more and more anxious about not sleeping with every seemingly week-length hour that creaks by, and then arrive feeling like I have been given the wrong size eyeballs, as well as being dehydrated and (odds are good) lacking one crucial charger, document, or garment that I have come to realize is home by the bed.

As a teen, I once flew with my parents to Italy on a business trip of my father's. We traveled on one of the aforementioned convenient overnight flights, a standard means of getting from the East Coast of the United States to Europe. We landed and headed for the business colleague's lovely residence, where a lovely meal had been prepared for us in the lovely dining room. It was presented as lunch, a concept that was in that moment unfamiliar to my stomach, which was still hovering somewhere south of Greenland. I felt unlovely in every respect, but there we were, at an elegant table, everything sauced just right and polished just so. My mother delivered an urgent, *sotto voce* table manners refresher course into my left ear as each item was brought to the table. "Quick, the napkin! Small fork! Spoon in other hand!" As this unspooled, I made meaningful eye contact with an orange in the fruit bowl on the sideboard, and began to understand that all I needed from life in that moment was contained within its lovely, bumpy skin.

Could I have it? Could I have the juicy orange, no doubt equal measures tart and sweet, to cut through the paste coating my inner workings? Our hostess saw me ogling the citrus and offered it to me. She smiled. I smiled. My mother smiled, too—then muttered urgently out of the corner of her mouth that was nearest to me, "Pretty sure you are expected to eat that with a knife and fork. We're in *Italy*." Salvation had been so close! I stared at the orange in defeat and announced I would save it for later, not realizing that stashing a snack in my room was probably equally barbaric-seeming to people who did not eat their fruit like monkeys at the table.

It's small wonder babies howl on airplanes, even when their ears are clear. We grow out of the freedom to express it so volubly (most of us, anyway) but we all still want to howl I think. Maybe you love to travel. Still, uprooting people and jangling their nerves and digestion by setting them down far from the things they like for breakfast and changing the tempo of the rhythms of their days and nights—it has an effect. They don't necessarily need the foods they are used to, but they do need to start out with foods that will set them upright again.

Laurie Colwin writes compellingly about the challenges and satisfactions to be found in selecting just the right thing to offer hungry people who have been battered by transit. Discussing a person just in from the airport after a long flight, she muses:

> *This person must be coddled, comforted and made to know that something delicious but not taxing will be waiting for him to eat . . . The question is, What? There are certain things a jet-lagged person should never be given. Complicated pastry, such as a napoleon, should never even be shown to people who have been in an airport within the past ten hours. Nor should they be offered steak or grilled meat. An omelet sounds right but is in fact wrong.*

She continues to mull the options, eventually crafting a small meal that will heal all "the little injuries and indignities of air travel." I read this with rapt attention when I first stumbled across it. I didn't know anyone else who obsessed to quite this degree, or derived the same happiness from getting it just right.

The little injuries and indignities of air travel have hardly subsided since Colwin put these words to paper, which was around the time I faced down the uncooperative citrus fruit. Thirty years of intervening progress mean a traveler's nerves and constitution are more prone to jangling and disorientation than ever. Despite all the technological advances and the dizzying array of airport foodstuffs now available (cheesecake in a cone! I saw it with my own eyes!), your recently arrived diner is even more likely to wash up on your doorstep feeling hungry and zonked, and still should not have to look at a napoleon. An arrival meal that addresses the dry, jangly feeling and does not overuse the mind or digits (one utensil, maximum) is just the ticket—a mug of soup and a sandwich with a bright little salad, say. Fresh fruit (an orange!) has always seemed especially restorative to me after a long flight, maybe because it strikes me as the antithesis of the dry, plasticky, jostling experience of being in an airplane. Just please present it peeled and ready to eat, even to an Italian.

Like short-term travelers, persons whose relocation is due to a more durable change of address, such as a new house, are going to need some dinner when they touch down. They may not have changed time zones or altitudes en route, but they have probably done substantially more packing, and are probably exponentially more disoriented. Moving houses is the literal definition of "unsettling," and calls for hearty fare to encourage new root growth.

At times of stress, of distress, of worry and fretting, I always think of Lillian and Russell Hoban's Frances the Badger and hear her calling out urgently, "I need my tiny special blanket!" Which we all do. In an airplane or on the ground, if we are older than about five and younger than about eighty-five, we are generally expected to modulate our needy demands and soldier onward, but at about dinnertime in a house full of boxes, a house still echoing weirdly, where none of the codes have been established or memorized, where no one can reach for anything without meditating on where it might be, I think you can kind of hear everyone calling out mournfully, if only on the inside, "I need my tiny special blanket!"

Search around for ideas for moving-day food and you'll find a lot of, "Go ahead and order a pizza—it's moving day!" But if you, kind friend or neighbor, are in a position to short-circuit that endeavor and deliver something healthy and substantial, something that will make the house smell like home, and so by extension begin to *feel* like home, then you will have done the kind of good deed that pizza, for all its charms, can scarcely dream of achieving.

Many years ago, when I was single and a city dweller, some friends moved into my neighborhood. I swung by on my way to a work function with a welcoming lasagna. "There's dinner handled!" Or so I thought. After the work function, I swung back. My friends, disoriented, exhausted, and ravenous from a day of moving, had followed the smell of hot lasagna to the oven area, where they were confronted with nine moving boxes marked KITCHEN. They eventually gave up trying to locate forks, plates, spatula, and oven mitts. Table forensics established that they had pulled the lasagna from the oven with a pair of boxer shorts, then (napkins in laps at least, one hopes) scooped it from the pan with teacups, out of which they guzzled it directly.

I learned two things from this episode: people who are moving should be gently encouraged to pack one box marked FIRST NIGHT with everything required to get from bedtime through breakfast (toothbrushes, coffee maker, clean socks, and so on), and moving-in meals should always include the objects and utensils required for semicivilized consumption, just in case.

SOOTHING GREEN BISQUE

This soup is easy on the senses, creamy enough to soothe, but not too heavy.

SERVES 4 TO 6

2–3 leeks

2 tablespoons olive oil, plus more to serve

10 ounces frozen corn kernels, or kernels from about 6 ears of fresh corn

Pinch of saffron threads, or

¼ teaspoon mild curry powder

Pinch of orange zest

½ cup full-fat canned coconut milk or half-and-half

2 cups chicken or vegetable stock

5–6 handfuls (about 5 ounces) baby spinach leaves

Salt

Minced chives, to serve (optional)

1 Trim tough ends and outer leaves from the leeks, wash grit from between the layers, and slice them finely. There should be 1½ cups.

2 Heat the olive oil over medium heat. Sauté the leeks, stirring frequently, for about 8 minutes, until softened. Add the corn and sauté for a few minutes, then add the saffron threads and orange zest.

3 Stir, add the coconut milk, and simmer for 2–3 minutes, then add the stock. Bring the mixture to a simmer and add the spinach. Cook for 2–3 minutes, until the greens are wilted but still bright. Remove from the heat and puree the soup until smooth.

4 Salt just to taste; start with ½ teaspoon. You can serve this warm or chilled, with a dribble of olive oil on top and a sprinkle of chives if desired. It will keep for 3–5 days refrigerated or frozen up to 3 months.

Now and Later
Buckwheat Cheese Puffs

These are basically popovers or, over on the continent, gougères. My son calls them "those hot little cheesy biscuits." But whatever you call them, they are easier to make than you think. They are most easily made in a stand mixer but are not much more trouble to mix by hand, and knowing this fact can make you the hero of a vacation week in a kitchen far from home, since the ingredients are pretty simple and all you really need is a pot and a spoon to produce them. You can mix the dough as far ahead as is practical in your life, because the prepared dough freezes (and bakes from frozen) like a dream, and it's well suited to doubling. So you can, for example, bring your new neighbors some baked ones for immediate snarfing and a tray of frozen ones to bake later, when they figure out how the oven works in the new place (the Now and Later Pumpkin Muffins, page 70, employ similar tactics). The gluten-free flour mix here gives them a nice earthy quality that complements the cheesiness without overburdening the little dears with virtuous heft. They make excellent teeny tiny sandwiches, with a smear of chutney or grainy mustard and a little ham or cheese. So concludes my ode to the cheese puff. Wear them in good health.

MAKES ABOUT 2 DOZEN

For
GLUTEN-FREE CHEESE PUFFS

1¼ cup (200g) sweet
  rice flour

¼ cup (44g) buckwheat
  flour

For
CONVENTIONAL CHEESE PUFFS

1½ cups (188g) all-
  purpose wheat flour

¼ cup (44g) buckwheat
  flour

For
BOTH CHEESE PUFFS

Pinch of cayenne
  and/or dry mustard
  powder, or freshly
  ground pepper

1 cup water	4 eggs	or a mixture), coarsely
½ cup (1 stick)	4 ounces sharp cheese	grated (about 1½
unsalted butter	(such as aged Gouda,	cups)
½ teaspoon salt	sharp cheddar, asiago,	

1   Preheat the oven to 425°F, and line two baking sheets with parchment paper.

2   Mix your flours of choice and spices together in a small bowl and reserve.

3   In a heavy medium saucepan, bring the water, butter, and salt to a boil over medium heat. Dump in the reserved dry mixture all in one go, and stir vigorously with a wooden spoon. It should all come together in a lumpy mass.

4   Lower the heat, and stir the lump around for a couple of minutes to dry it out a little. Don't fret over the bit that sticks to the pan.

5   Remove the lump to the bowl of a stand mixer fitted with the paddle attachment, and beat it for a minute on its own to let some of the steamier heat escape (or just stir it in the pan, off the heat, if you choose to do the thing by hand).

6   Now one at a time, crack each egg into a small cup (this prevents the very sad accident of dropping an egg shell into the path of the beaters) and add it to the bowl, beating well after each egg. The dough is still hot enough to cook the eggs on contact, so you really want to be sure to beat, beat, beat once the egg is added. It may look dire at various points while you are adding the eggs, but keep the faith and

recipe continues

keep mixing to incorporate each egg well before you add the next, and by the end you should have a thick, shiny mass. Scrape the bowl down after the last egg has been incorporated and beat for 30 seconds more.

7 Using a spatula, fold in most of the cheese, reserving a little bit to sprinkle on top.

8 To shape the cheese puffs, I prefer to use two spoons. You can make teeny little puffs (using teaspoons) or bigger puffs (using soup spoons). Using your chosen spoons, plop the dough in little mounds a few inches apart onto the prepared baking sheets. Slide into the hot oven, and bake for about 10 minutes, until puffed and golden all over. Now reduce the heat to 375°F, rotate the sheets in the oven, and bake for another 10–15 minutes, until the puffs are deeper golden and firm to the touch. If you will be holding them for someone's arrival (or departure) or transporting them to someone else's house and don't want them to collapse (as waiting often leads to), you can poke a vent hole into the side of each puff with a small skewer, and leave them in the turned-off, door-cracked oven to cool slowly.

9 To freeze for later baking, plop the dough blobs onto a parchment-lined tray and move to the freezer. Allow them to freeze solid, a matter of a couple hours, then wrap in a tightly sealed bag to store. If you are baking from frozen you don't need to thaw them, but you should add a few minutes to the baking time.

10 These are best the day they are baked, but can be stored at room temperature for a day or two, and refreshed with a few minutes in a hot oven before eating.

LETTUCE CUPS

*Lettuce cups are a handy way to get the protein and the salad into the people all at once, without a need for utensils, which makes them well suited to stand-up eating in between loads from the van or jet-lagged consumption when a person does not remember in which hand they hold the fork in this time zone. Cherry tomatoes are not super delicious year-round, but they are more reliable out of season than regular tomatoes, and they respond really well to roasting, after which they **are** super delicious year-round. Any protein works for this, making it easy to customize for all stripes of diner.*

SERVES 4 TO 6

1 pint cherry tomatoes

3 teaspoons olive oil, divided

1 teaspoon maple syrup

¼ teaspoon coarse salt

Freshly ground pepper

4 ounces grilled tofu or meat (chicken, beef, or pork), or ½ cup roasted almonds

½ cup fresh basil leaves

3–5 scallions, white and lighter green parts only

1 navel, blood, or Cara Cara orange

1 firm-ripe avocado

1 small head Boston or Bibb lettuce, 1 romaine heart, or 2 heads of endive, washed and dried

1   Preheat the oven to 375°F, and line a small baking dish with parchment paper.

2   Using a small sharp knife, slice the cherry tomatoes in half and lay them cut side up in the baking dish. Drizzle or brush the tops of the tomatoes with 2 teaspoons of the olive oil, followed by the

recipe continues

maple syrup, salt, and a generous twist of pepper. Roast for about 25 minutes, until the tomatoes wrinkle and condense. Transfer to a medium bowl and let them cool their jets while you prepare the rest of the ingredients.

3   Chop or shred the protein you have selected. Chop the basil. Mince the scallions quite finely. Add all of these to the bowl.

4   Segment or supreme the orange: using that same sharp knife, cut off the stem and blossom ends so the orange stands helpfully on the cutting board, then slice the peel off in strips, from top to bottom, just inside the white pith, repeating and turning until it is naked before you. Working over the bowl, use the knife to remove the segments from the membranes, letting them fall, then squeeze the last of the juice from the orange into the bowl as well, and toss lightly with the other ingredients.

5   Halve and pit the avocado and dice it into ½-inch cubes, adding it straight to the bowl to get coated in the orange juice.

6   Add the remaining 1 teaspoon olive oil, and adjust the salt to your taste.

7   If you are packing this for delivery, stack the washed lettuce leaves in damp paper towels or dishcloths in a lidded container or zip bag, and pack the salad separately. At serving time, scoop a ¼ cup of the mixture into the bowl of the lettuce leaves, which can be arranged on a platter or dish.

BLACK BEAN SOUP

A big pot of beans is my kind of food. Beans are cheap to assemble, easy to prepare, and improve upon reheating (so much so that I try not to serve this soup until its second or third day of life). As a soup, this plays well with cornbread, rice, or baked potatoes. Thickened, which it does naturally as it stands, it becomes an ingredient for burritos or a topping for nachos. By providing a household with a vat of this stuff for dinner—along with a big bag of tortilla chips, some already shredded cheese, and a jar of salsa—you'll be setting them up to eat for days. On day one, they eat the soup with the chips and cheese on top, and on day two, they eat the chips with the soup and cheese on top, an experience that harmonizes nicely with trying to fit the sofa into the new floorplan.

Regarding chipotle peppers, which I recommend adding if you want some extra heat, it's my habit to buy a can or jar of them and dump it into a small freezer-safe container. They don't freeze solid, making it easy to extract all or part of one whenever their smoky heat is called for. Note that it's best to soak the beans overnight (cover generously in water and add a pinch of baking soda) before making the soup, so you will need to factor in that time.

SERVES 4 TO 6

3 cups dry black beans, soaked overnight and drained

¼ cup olive oil

1 large or 2 medium yellow onions, finely chopped (about 1½ cups)

4 cloves garlic, minced

2 tablespoons ancho chili powder

4 teaspoons ground cumin

2 teaspoons crushed dried oregano

One 28-ounce can plain diced or ground tomatoes

6 cups water

Large handful of fresh cilantro, chopped

½ to 1 chipotle pepper in adobo sauce (optional; see headnote)

One 4-ounce can roasted green chilies, chopped

2 teaspoons salt

recipe continues

To
SERVE
Grated cheddar or
  Monterey Jack cheese

Green salsa
Dollop of plain yogurt
Tortilla chips

1   Preheat the oven to 350°F.

2   In an ovenproof pot (I use my Dutch oven), heat the olive oil and sauté the onions over medium heat until they soften. Add the garlic, ancho chili powder, cumin, and oregano, and sauté for 1–2 minutes longer, until the fragrance is all around you. Add the beans, tomatoes, and water, stir well, and bring to a simmer.

3   Cover the pot, put it in the oven, and lower the heat to 250°F. Go on about your day. Stir if you feel like it, from time to time. After 2–3 hours, see if the beans are totally soft (this will depend on the age of your beans). Keep going if not. If they are, take the pot out and turn off the oven. You can pause the soup making at this point if you need to.

4   When you are ready to resume or continue, toss the cilantro and the chipotle pepper, if using, into the pot and use an immersion blender to partially blend the soup. It should be smooth-ish, but with texture. Add the green chilies and the salt, taste, and adjust to your liking.

5   The beans will keep for at least 5 days refrigerated. The more times you let this mixture cool and then reheat it, the more the texture will improve and the flavors will deepen. You can also freeze this soup for up to 3 months.

TWICE-BAKED POTATOES

As my friend Suzi says, there's logistics, and then there's living through it.
If logistics are a big driver of your life, you probably know that things that
ought to work in sequence often end up becoming a story you'll be able to laugh
at someday. There are also little gifts that your idle self can give your busy self
when she comes around later looking for something to eat. If at any point you
find yourself with the oven on for some other purpose or you just find yourself
at home for an hour or so, bake some potatoes. They can be baking potatoes or
Yukon Gold potatoes or purple sweet potatoes or yams. I don't care unless you
do. Cool them down and tuck them away. The next time the universe presents
you with 20 minutes to spare, split the potatoes and scrape them out and load
them with all kinds of nutritious tidbits, then bake them again. Now you've
done something pretty great. Now humans dashing around at high speeds
can grab one of these items and be pretty well sustained. With a salad and
maybe some soup, seated people can call them dinner. They are tasty at room
temperature and comforting when warmed up again, which they tolerate well,
so you can even tuck the finished product away for another future crunch. This
is one way to do them; I've listed some other ideas after the recipe.

SERVES 4

4 large yams or sweet
potatoes
2 cups shredded or
baby kale, washed but
not dried
1 small bunch scallions,
ends trimmed and

tough outer layers
removed
2 teaspoons olive or
sesame oil
1 tablespoon sesame
seeds
2–3 teaspoons tamari
or soy sauce

1 cup buttermilk or
plain Greek yogurt
4 ounces Monterey
Jack cheese, grated
(1 cup), divided
Freshly ground pepper

recipe continues

1   Preheat the oven to 350°F. Prick the potatoes with a fork or score them with a small X and bake them for about 45 minutes, until tender. If you are planning to do all the steps in one go, leave the oven on but do your hands a favor and let the potatoes cool a little before proceeding.

2   When you can interact with the potatoes without altering your fingerprints, slice them in half the long way and scrape most but not all of the flesh out into a bowl (leave about ¼ inch of potato in the peel). Mash this a bit, and reserve. Arrange the potato boats on a baking dish lined with foil or parchment.

3   Wilt the greens over medium heat in a small covered skillet with the water that still clings from washing; remove to a small bowl.

4   Mince the scallions and add them to the pan with the oil, sesame seeds, and tamari. Increase the heat a bit until you hear a sizzle, then return the greens to the pan and stir and fry for about 2 minutes, until the leaves are nicely coated.

5   Add the buttermilk to the reserved potato flesh and stir to combine, then stir in the cooked greens and ½ cup of the cheese, along with a few twists of pepper.

6   Portion this among the potato shells and sprinkle the remaining ½ cup cheese over the tops. You can pause there, refrigerating until a later baking time, or pop them back in the hot oven and bake for about 15 minutes, until the tops are golden.

7   Serve hot, or cool the baked potatoes to room temperature and allow foragers to help themselves. If you will be storing them for the next day or for transport, make sure they have cooled before closing them into a lidded container. They reheat nicely in a toaster oven

or regular oven; about 10 minutes at 350° will crisp and warm them enough for snarfing if they have been refrigerated. They will keep, covered tightly in the refrigerator, for up to 3 days.

OTHER WAYS TO DO IT

- ADD AN ADDITIONAL ½ CUP FINELY MINCED STEAMED GREENS PER POTATO. TRY ANY COMBINATION OF SPINACH, KALE, CHARD, OR OTHER FAVORITE GREEN.

- ADD 1 TABLESPOON PER POTATO OF GOLDEN FLAX MEAL OR OAT BRAN.

- SUBSTITUTE THE BUTTERMILK WITH COCONUT MILK, CASHEW CREAM, OR BROTH.

- SUBSTITUTE THE JACK CHEESE WITH ANY OTHER GRATED, SHARP CHEESE, OR CRUMBLED FETA.

- ADD 1 TABLESPOON PER POTATO OF ANY LITTLE NUBBIN THAT SEEMS SAVORY AND APPEALING, SUCH AS CAPERS, OLIVES, MINCED HAM OR BACON, OR SMOKED TOFU.

- SEASON WITH PAPRIKA, CUMIN, CHILI, OR CURRY POWDER TO TASTE.

RED RICE

with
SQUASH AND SMOKY CHEESE

Oh, nothing to see here, just rice and squash—but something incredibly hearty and satisfying happens when they get together with the smoky cheese and peppers, something that makes a house smell like home and bellies feel content.

SERVES 4 TO 6

2 cups red rice

1 medium red onion

2–3 tablespoons olive oil, divided

1 teaspoon cumin seeds

1 small butternut squash (about 1½ pounds)

2 teaspoons maple syrup

Salt and freshly ground pepper

All or part of 1 chipotle pepper in adobo sauce, finely minced (see the note on page 59)

5 ounces smoked cheddar, cut in ½-inch cubes

Chutney, to serve (optional)

1 Rinse the rice briefly and drain. Combine the rice with water to generously cover in a medium saucepan and bring to a boil. Lower the heat and cover the pot. Cook for 40 minutes, until the rice is just tender. Drain any excess water, cover the pot, and let stand for 10 minutes. Fluff it with a fork or rice paddle and set it aside to cool enough that it won't melt the cheese on contact when you combine everything.

2 Preheat the oven to 400°F, and line a baking sheet with parchment paper.

3   Peel the onion, and chop it into ½-inch pieces. Combine the onion with 1 tablespoon of the olive oil and the cumin seeds in a medium bowl and toss until evenly coated. Spread the onion bits out on one half of the prepared baking sheet.

4   Peel and seed the squash, and dice it into ½-inch cubes. In the same bowl you used for the onion, toss the squash with 1 tablespoon of the olive oil, the maple syrup, ½ teaspoon of salt, and a few twists of pepper. Spread it in a single layer on the other side of the baking sheet. Roast the onion and squash in the oven, stirring gently from time to time, 15–20 minutes. Keeping the two segregated allows you to pull one or the other if their cooking rates are out of sync. You want them both to be tender and lightly browned. Let the vegetables cool a few minutes.

5   Turn the oven down to 350°F. Lightly oil a 9 × 13-inch baking dish.

6   Toss the cooked vegetables with the cooked rice and the chipotle pepper in a large bowl. Adjust seasoning with salt and pepper (don't forget to factor in the saltiness of your cheese) and add a little more olive oil if needed so that every grain has a nice light sheen. Toss the cheese with the rice and vegetables, and transfer to the prepared baking dish. Bake for about 25 minutes, until any cheese cubes visible on top are golden. Serve hot or at warm room temperature. A little chutney wouldn't hurt, alongside at serving time. To reheat, slide the dish into a 325°F oven, uncovered, and warm it through. This will keep for up to 3 days, covered tightly and refrigerated.

SALAD FOR A HOT NIGHT IN A NEW PLACE

If hummus and tabbouleh salad fell apart into their component pieces, I think this is what would result. With protein, vegetables, and a savory zip, this salad is a satisfying restorative after a sweaty day of schlepping things here and there.

SERVES 4 TO 6

½ cup quinoa

3 cups cooked, drained chickpeas (about 1 cup dry beans, soaked and cooked, or two 15-ounce cans, rinsed)

1–3 cloves garlic

½ teaspoon kosher salt

¼ cup olive oil

2 tablespoons Preserved Lemon Puree (recipe follows)

3 tablespoons zatar, or 1 tablespoon cumin + 1 tablespoon sesame seeds

1 cup minced fresh parsley

1 medium tomato (or equivalent amount of cherry tomatoes), chopped (about 1 cup)

Juice of 1 lemon

6 handfuls (about 5 ounces) baby kale, romaine, or arugula, washed and dried

To SERVE

1 tablespoon olive oil

1–2 tablespoons fresh lemon juice

1 tablespoon Preserved Lemon Puree

1 Rinse the quinoa briefly and place it in a small pot with water to cover generously. Bring to a boil and then simmer, partially covered, for about 15 minutes, until almost tender. Drain off most of the water and cover the pot snugly, placing it over the lowest flame to steam until fully cooked. Remove the lid, fluff with a fork, and leave to cool.

2 Spread the chickpeas on a paper towel or a clean kitchen towel and pat them dry; the more you dry them, the crispier they will get in the oil and the less they will spit at you while it happens.

3 Using the flat side of your knife, smash the garlic cloves against the cutting board, then chop the salt into them, continuing to mash and chop until you have a lovely, smooth paste.

4 Heat the olive oil in a heavy skillet set over medium heat until it ripples. Cook the chickpeas for 5–7 minutes, until they are a golden toasty brown all over. That golden crust is the main attraction. Insist upon it.

5 Remove the pan from the heat and add the garlic paste and the preserved lemon to the chickpeas. Stir this all together in the residual heat of the pan for about 1 minute. Now add the zatar and toss to combine. Remove to a bowl, and let cool for a few minutes. Toss with the reserved quinoa, parsley, tomatoes, and lemon juice, and allow to sit for 5 minutes; taste and adjust with as much additional seasoning as you need to make it irresistible.

6 Spread the baby greens on a small platter and heap the chickpea mixture on top. Serve warm or allow to cool to room temperature.

7 The flavors tend to mellow as they stand. Combine the olive oil, lemon juice, and Preserved Lemon Puree in a small jar, and send along for last-minute dressing.

PRESERVED LEMON PUREE

I use a lot of preserved lemons. I am basically always trying to keep a rein on the impulse to say, how about we add a little preserved lemon to that? My friend Julie taught me to make preserved lemons many years ago. Her method includes a tiny bit of sugar, which sounds wrong until either you meet Julie (whereupon you grasp instantly that she has the right ideas) or remember the value of balance in all things. The sugar basically disappears, just working quietly in the background. I have tried and tested at least six ways to make preserved lemons, but I always come back to Julie's formula—3 parts salt to ½ part sugar—as the base. For variation, consider including a blood orange or kumquat in among the lemons; a teaspoon of Korean gochujang chili paste or ground dried red pepper (the type sold for making kimchi), or dried Aleppo pepper all give a gentle kick of heat.

MAKES 2 PINTS

¾ cup kosher salt	3–5 organic lemons	2–3 additional lemons
2 tablespoons sugar	(Meyer are best),	(not Meyer), for
	washed, to preserve	additional juice

1 Sterilize two pint-size glass jars with tight-sealing, noncorrosive lids.

2 Combine the salt and sugar in a small shallow bowl.

3 Slice the organic lemons crossways, about ½-inch thick, and use the knife tip to flick the seeds aside. Press a slice into the salt mixture and then drop it, salt-side-down, into the jar. Continue for the rest of the sliced lemons, stacking the slices salt-side-down, until the jar is full to the first thread, jamming a few slices around the column if the diameter of the jar permits. Let these stand for 3 hours and up to overnight, covered, at room temperature. A good amount of juice should have accumulated, but in all likelihood, it will not come all the way up to the top of the stack. Juice your regular lemons and strain this juice into the jars so that the juice covers the top lemon slice.

4   Now wait. Leave the jars on a tray or plate in a corner of your kitchen, where their bright color and promise of good things to come entices you to hold the jars and turn the jars and give them some admiration and also mild agitation every few days. In about 3 weeks (there is too much acid and salt in these jars for anything bad to happen at room temperature, I promise), the lemons should be utterly soft. If your kitchen is warm, this may happen faster; if your kitchen is cool, you may want to leave them another week.

5   When the lemons are fully transformed, dump the contents of the jars into your food processor or blender and pulse to make a thick slurry, before returning them to the jar. Do this for two reasons: it is recipe-ready at all times with no fuss from that time forward, and you get to make salad dressing in the blender with the dregs. These keep for months in the refrigerator.

NOW AND LATER PUMPKIN MUFFINS

The notion of the stuffed muffin—in this case, part pumpkin bread and part cheesecake—came my way from Alanna Taylor-Tobin, the genius pastry chef and food stylist behind The Bojon Gourmet. I jumped when she put out a call for recipe testers for her book, Alternative Baker, and thanks to a combination of deadlines (hers), insomnia (mine), and compatibly obsessive personalities, as well as a three-hour time difference, we built a bridge of baked goods from coast to coast. Just like the Cheese Puffs on page 54, these muffins bake from frozen like champs, so do this: bake half the recipe for your recipients, and tuck the remainder into one of those foil six-cup muffin pans from the supermarket; stash them in the recipient's freezer for a time to come when they are mentally prepared to use the oven. It probably bears saying that there's nothing to stop you from loading your own freezer with these muffins, as a kind of hospitality insurance.

MAKES 1 DOZEN MUFFINS

For the
FILLING

5 ounces plain fresh
goat cheese, at room
temperature

¼ cup sugar

1 tablespoon sweet
rice flour (substitute
all-purpose flour for
conventional muffins)

1 egg yolk (reserve the
white for the muffins)

1 tablespoon sour
cream or plain yogurt

1 tablespoon lemon
juice

½ teaspoon vanilla
extract

Pinch of salt

For
GLUTEN-FREE MUFFINS

½ cup (80g) sweet rice
flour

1 cup (90g) oat flour

½ cup + 1 tablespoon
(40g) tapioca flour

¼ cup (30g) millet flour

For
CONVENTIONAL MUFFINS

Scant 2 cups (240g)
all-purpose flour

For
BOTH MUFFINS

½ cup ghee or coconut
oil, at soft room
temperature (or
melted and cooled)

¾ cup squash puree or
canned pure pumpkin

⅓ cup buttermilk

⅔ cup packed brown or
unrefined sugar

1 tablespoon molasses

1 egg white

1 egg

1½ teaspoons baking
powder

¼ teaspoon baking
soda

½ teaspoon salt

1 teaspoon ground
cinnamon

1 teaspoon ground
ginger

¼ teaspoon ground
coriander

⅛ teaspoon freshly
grated nutmeg

¼ cup hemp hearts or
oat bran

1 Preheat the oven to 350°F if you plan to bake these right away. Line a standard twelve-cup muffin pan with muffin liners, or lightly butter or spray the cups.

2 Prepare the filling. In a small bowl, beat the goat cheese and sugar together until smooth. Add the flour, egg yolk, sour cream, lemon juice, vanilla, and salt, and combine thoroughly. Set aside while you prepare the muffins.

3 Whisk together the ghee, squash puree, buttermilk, sugar, molasses, and eggs in a medium bowl.

4 Sift together the baking powder, baking soda, salt, cinnamon, ginger, coriander, nutmeg, and hemp hearts in a large bowl. Make a well in the center of this mixture, and gently fold in the wet ingredients until just combined. Batter will be thick. Divide the batter evenly between the muffin cups.

recipe continues

5   Use the back of an ordinary teaspoon to make a small well in the center of each muffin, and then spoon the filling in, about 1 tablespoon per cup.

6   If you are baking right away, slide the muffin pan onto the center rack of the oven and bake for about 30 minutes, until puffed and golden.

7   For muffins you are saving for later, slide the muffin pan into the freezer, and freeze until solid before sealing them well to protect them from freezer burn. The night before baking, move the muffin pan to the fridge to thaw overnight, and bake as above, adding perhaps 5 minutes to the baking time to allow for the chill.

8   Cooled muffins can be wrapped in foil or tucked into a napkin-lined basket for transport. These are tastiest the day they are baked, but they're also delicious split in half and toasted on days two and three.

LIFE IS UPSIDE-DOWN CAKE

This is a great cake to have up your sleeve even when your life is right-side up. Without the fruit and caramel, it is a very tasty layer cake if you bump into a birthday or other similar occasion, and a tweak here and there will give you, for example, a lemon–poppy seed cake. But as is true for most of us, this cake's true mettle is revealed when life turns it upside down (and gives it caramel). Underneath (which will eventually become the top), any number of sliced fruits work beautifully: rhubarb, apples, peaches, plums, pears, even thin slices of orange and lemon (with their peels intact).

MAKES ONE 9-INCH ROUND CAKE

For the
FRUIT AND CARAMEL

4 tablespoons unsalted butter
⅓ cup sugar
2 tablespoons honey
½ teaspoon lemon zest
¼ teaspoon salt
1 teaspoon finely grated fresh ginger
2 tablespoons sake or mirin
1 teaspoon lemon juice
4 large peaches or other fruit (see headnote), peeled and sliced

For
GLUTEN-FREE CAKE

1 cup (90g) oat flour
½ cup (80g) sweet rice flour

For
CONVENTIONAL CAKE

1⅓ cups (170g) all-purpose flour

For
BOTH CAKES

¾ cup (1½ sticks) unsalted butter, softened

3½ ounces (100g) cooked, peeled chestnuts (see headnote)
¾ cup sugar
2 eggs, room temperature
2 teaspoons vanilla extract
Finely grated zest of ½ lemon (about 1 teaspoon)
1 teaspoon baking powder
½ teaspoon baking soda
½ teaspoon salt
¼ cup buttermilk

recipe continues

Precooked, prepeeled chestnuts, surely a prizewinning innovation, are increasingly available in average grocery stores, and absolutely and reliably available in Asian groceries. You can substitute an equivalent weight of almond or hazelnut paste if chestnuts are not easily found in your vicinity. Having all your ingredients at room temperature yields a smooth batter, so leave time for that.

1   Preheat the oven to 350°F, and ensure your rack is in the center of the oven. Lightly butter a 9-inch round cake tin, line it with a circle of parchment, and then butter the parchment.

2   Prepare the caramel. Melt the butter in a heavy saucepan. Stir in the sugar, honey, lemon zest, salt, and ginger, and cook over medium-high heat until it is smooth and beginning to bubble. Slowly add the sake and lemon juice; adding it quickly could lead to a flaming mess, so pour with care. Continue to cook, stirring, for 2 minutes, until the mixture is well amalgamated and bubbling thickly. Only the heat of this lava-temperature substance prevents ~~me~~ you from eating it all before the cake is made.

3   Pour the mixture into the waiting pan, tilting to make an even layer. Allow this to cool a few minutes before arranging the fruit on top of it.

4   Prepare the cake. Put the butter, chestnuts, and sugar into the bowl of a food processor; pulse to coarsely combine, then run the machine, periodically pausing to scrape the sides, until well creamed. Add the eggs one at a time, thoroughly combining and scraping after each, then add the vanilla and lemon zest.

5   Add the flour(s), baking powder, baking soda, and salt to the bowl and pulse five or six times to incorporate. Scrape again, add the buttermilk, and pulse until just blended.

6   Glop the batter over the fruit mixture and gently even it out as best you can, trying not to disturb the fruit layer. It is pretty remarkable how messily you can do this and still have the cake emerge presentable—it smooths out quite a lot as it bakes.

7   Bake for 40–50 minutes, until the top is uniformly golden and the sides are beginning to pull away from the pan. If the top is browning too quickly, turn the oven down to 325°F for the last 20 minutes of baking.

8   Set the pan on a rack to cool for up to 15 minutes, and then loosen the edges with a thin spatula or knife. Fit a plate over the pan, and using oven mitts, ninja skills, and careful attention, hold the plate firmly to the pan and turn the cake upside down. Listen for the sigh as the cake plops onto the plate. Remove the pan and peel off the parchment. Perform any necessary minor adjustments if some fruit has been displaced. Allow the cake to cool—the cooler it is, the more it holds together, a lesson to us all I suppose—before covering securely for transport.

3

FOOD
FOR ILLNESS
AND
RECOVERY

WHEN ONCE IT IS RECOGNIZED

that it is those who have
been the most carefully fed
and nourished who make
the most speedy recovery,

A KNOWLEDGE OF
INVALID COOKING
WILL BE ESTIMATED
AT ITS PROPER VALUE.

FLORENCE B. JACK,
The Good Housekeeping
Invalid Cookery Book (1926)

IN 1939, A PEDIATRICIAN FROM CHICAGO NAMED CLARA DAVIS PUBLISHED THE RESULTS OF A TOTALLY BIZARRE STUDY SHE HAD DEVISED USING THE BABIES AND YOUNG CHILDREN OF TEENAGE MOTHERS, WIDOWS, AND OTHERS TOO POOR TO FEED THEIR CHILDREN WELL. FIFTEEN SUBJECTS WERE ENTRUSTED TO HER CARE AND IN RETURN FOR THE PROMISE TO FEED THEM, THEY WERE HOUSED IN A KIND OF NUTRITIONAL ORPHANAGE. THERE THEY WERE OFFERED, WITHOUT URGING OR DIRECTION OF ANY KIND, AN ARRAY OF FOOD CHOICES. EACH FOOD WAS PRESENTED IN A VERY SIMPLE STATE, EACH IN A SEPARATE LITTLE BOWL, AND THE BOWLS ARRANGED IN ROWS ON A TRAY. THE SUPERVISING ADULTS DID NO SMILING OR COOING OR MAKING OF AIRPLANE NOISES, HANDS-DOWN THE MOST DISTURBING DETAIL OF THE STUDY TO ME WHEN I THINK OF THE LITTLE BEINGS IN THEIR CARE. THE PRECISE AMOUNT OF EVERY SINGLE THING THE SUBJECTS GRABBED, SPILLED, ATE, AND SUBSEQUENTLY ELIMINATED WAS RECORDED AND ANALYZED.

What she found was that, presented with healthy options and left alone to decide, babies and children could be trusted to construct a balanced diet on their own. They might binge on one food group for a spell, but overall they tended toward balance in the diets they constructed for themselves. Even more notably, babies who were deficient in some nutrient (like vitamin D, for example) gravitated toward foods that naturally contained it (such as cod liver oil, which to hear my mother tell it, is not especially delicious on its own).

Davis likened children's instinctive appetite for what is necessary to meet their present physical needs to the manner in which a body's autonomic systems adjust to external cues. Autonomy is a beautiful thing for a body, accounting for the fact that most of us do not need to remind ourselves to sweat when we are hot, or to breathe faster when we exert ourselves, or to duck when something flies toward our heads.

But the autonomy in our appetites is something we lose touch with. By the time we've reached maturity, bombarded as we are with a dizzying variety of philosophies and options, it can be hard to get in touch with the guiding light within. This is where sickness can be a kind of ally, because it is pretty revealing.

The thing I've noticed paying close attention to feeding people who are making use of the calories in meaningful ways, like growing children and pregnant people and anyone who is grappling with illness, is that the more your body needs something, the more likely you are to find it appealing. I am not referring here to the urge to eat a doughnut; that is another principle entirely. But take the case of the Slippery Soup. A friend of mine whose vocal cords were giving her trouble at an inconvenient time professionally was told by a fancy doctor-to-the-stars that these cords of hers were exceptionally *parched*.

Something about this word, "parched," put me in mind of the Slippery Soup I would make for my children when they were small and had just emerged from one of those sudden and feverish little illnesses of childhood that blow through like a storm at sea and leave a small person droopy and dry and in need of restoration. The soup sounds kind of unappealing, I warned her, and though it doesn't contain anything intrinsically yucky (it is not made with innards, tentacles, or anything smelly), it's also not a very beautiful soup. But if it is the right stuff for you, I continued (remembering my flushed tots slurping it down), you'll probably find it tasty.

My friend made the soup. "What the heck are you making?" her appalled husband asked. But she could not answer him, because she was eating it up. Is this therefore the only soup anyone should feed people who are ill? No, it is not. But it was definitely the right food at the right time for that person.

This principle becomes perhaps even more important, and trickier to put into practice, when the illness at hand isn't just a passing cold but a more drawn-out business. When my oldest sister was first diagnosed with cancer, a wise advisor reminded me: your sister is a statistic of one. The things you read about the cancer she has, and about how patients respond to the treatments she selects, or how they fare when they don't have the treatments she declines, is informative but not wholly so. The holy truth for her is in her own experience. I think this was the most valuable line of thinking I took away from the two years of her illness. When you are feeding the patient, feed *that* patient. Accept what rules you must from outside sources, but above all, find a way to connect to the patient's pleasure and comfort and appetite, and work always toward that. That is true sustenance.

Accepting that all illnesses and also all patients are their own ecosystems, with different symptoms, sensitivities, responses, and preferences, it's still possible to say a few almost universal things about feeding illness and recovery.

An active phase of sickness calls for the most tolerable, pure, and minimalistic support. Not much quantity is usually required or desired to support a body in the thick of an acute stage of illness, but that little bit of nourishment is essential to fuel the body's healing response. With limited opportunities to get calories in, there's little latitude for serving empty ones. The potential significance of those meals only increases when you add in the fact that so much besides calories can be delivered on the tray that enters the sickroom. No pressure!

Over many years of looking after myself and then three children, I'd developed a mental file of food for the sickroom that served pretty well, tempting little bits of this and that to hydrate and sustain the patient. I wouldn't say that all of that was rendered irrelevant when my sister was facing down a terminal illness, but I had to reframe a good portion of it, starting with my confidence.

Throughout her cancer, food was a huge and fraught issue. There were particular foods and ingredients (fluid and salt, for example) that had to be avoided or limited due to her philosophies of healing or to straight-up doctor's orders. There were strong aversions brought on by treatments or symptoms, and there were deep cravings that could not be slaked for similar reasons. It was a minefield. The stakes were high, because her life literally depended on it and because both the pleasure of eating and strong beliefs about nutrition were core matters for her. Finally and most importantly, though, it was fraught because she was in so much pain. Anything that could feel good seemed so important to provide, and meals gave us many daily opportunities to try.

I learned many lessons I'd rather not have learned from tending to her during this period. The main one as far as food goes was this: tiny little normal things, as minor as a nicely folded napkin, are easy to overlook when the going gets rough to this degree. But they matter so much. I learned that it's important to make sickroom food look presentable not only because it is more appetizing, but also because maybe beauty and dining and other pleasures of upright, regular life have been lost in the sauce of sickness. I learned that the unbearable is made bearable by gestures like these, gestures that have more to do with love and insight than medicine or other practical considerations.

Speaking of universal truths, the worry and work imposed by the tasks of looking after someone are almost always compounded by worry over tasks in the rest of your life that are going unmet as a result, and together these can push aside anything that feels like a nicety. Caregivers, even family members, understandably feel a push to emphasize efficiency over other aspects of constructing sickroom meals. When she was caring for her father, the writer Edwidge Danticat wrote in the book *Brother, I'm Dying*, "I realized that for nearly a year, while my mother, brothers and I had constantly carried food up to my father, we had rarely eaten *with* him. Somehow it hadn't occurred to me that he missed sharing a table or a plate, passing a spice or a spoon." These are not superficial things she mentions. These are fundamental elements of existing as a person in community. They are endangered by illness, and essential to dignity, and we ought to protect them for as long as they are available. The first memories I clung to after my sister died revolved around the satisfying feeling of tracking down—often in some terribly unlikely places—what she wanted to eat, and sharing that table with her.

Eve Ensler wrote about the curve ball of appetite that cancer served her. A lifelong vegetarian, when she woke up from radical surgery she wanted—craved, demanded, *had to have*—a hamburger. "Meat had always repulsed me," she writes in *In the Body of the World*. "But now I was out for blood. I could have had fangs. I shocked myself and my friends [who] said it might be too much to go from a thimbleful of Jell-O to a hamburger. I said I felt a hamburger was my ticket back. They seemed disturbed, as if I was a lifelong Communist suddenly selling hedge funds. They needed me to be who I had always been for them. I said a lot of things had changed." Slippery Soup, hamburger, you name it—bodies make their needs known, if we listen, and that's what we ought to do.

Your patient may have a cold or flu or some other fleeting consideration, or a chronic complaint, something with overall lower stakes. Some of the same principles apply, though: food should still be a source of support, pleasure, and satisfaction, not chiefly a medicine, or a chore, or a pit of potential hazards to be navigated nervously. A beautiful dividend is that finding a way to connect to the pleasures of the food you are offering has benefits for everyone in the equation.

When he was little, my son used to have regular bouts of what we came to call Special Occasion Flu because it always seemed to coincide with ticketed events or big parties. It involved a fever and a lot of upheaval all over everything and was usually done with inside of eight hours. The only thing he could tolerate eating when the dust and laundry settled was miso soup. He's outgrown this thing, whatever it was, but he has trailed that element of recovery along as he grew. He is just not set to rights after any challenge until he has a bowl of miso soup.

Miso was also a thread that ran through the wilds of caring for my sister. Miso soup was what she called for when deep hunger rankled her system, when she was feeling too hungry and unwell to imagine anything else she might want to eat. After the soup, she could often imagine plenty of things she wanted to eat, but nothing but miso could move her from the one state to the other.

It was such a small detail in the storm, but one that connected me to home and to the caregiving energy that is at the nucleus of everything for me. Even in the strange, dark places cancer forced us all to explore, that familiar, briny whiff of the soup restored—if only a little bit—the ragged parts of me, too. "You can do this," said the soup. "We're carrying soup here, okay? Right now, your job is just to carry this soup, the same way you've done it a thousand times before."

In these unique ecosystems of patient and illness, the caregiver is a vital component. The motions of feeding and being fed are not so separate from the emotions. You don't really have to do anything about that, which is a relief since you can't, really, other than pay attention to it, and let the motions be a kind of meditation, and take plenty of extra breaths.

As to what is good for someone with this complaint or that one, I'll say that I have a basic skepticism about any orthodox belief system, but I do have an orthodox belief that very few things are unequivocally and universally good, or bad, for everybody. There is plenty of heated and conflicting dietary advice available in the world. I think if you keep things simple, and your eyes open ("You can observe a lot by watching," said the famous caregiver Yogi Berra), you will feed your humans well.

IN THE SICKROOM

The first group of recipes in this chapter is for people who are not much interested in (or able to handle) solid food. For most illnesses, this time is short-lived, or at least cyclical, and the food in the following group is more engineered toward recovery and restoration.

THE HOUSE MISO

This is a simple miso soup, very like the one that comes with your meal in just about any Japanese restaurant. Miso has a lot going for it: ease of preparation (provided you are well stocked with the staples, all of which conveniently boast a long shelf life), fundamental nutrition (protein, minerals, and hydration), and supreme digestibility (thanks to the ferment that gives miso its umami flavor). Miso is an excellent restorative: full of the electrolytes whose balance one may have thrown off (or up) while ill, rich in elemental forms of protein, and boasting plenty of other micronutrients and minerals to paste a person back together. There are legions of painstaking and complex and delicious ways to make a subtle, complex, and elegant miso soup. But when I have exhausted the supply of clean towels, or just exhausted myself, I do it in a very simple way.

4-6 SERVINGS

4 cups Dashi broth (recipe follows) and the kombu seaweed saved from that preparation

1 handful dried fueru wakame seaweed

2-3 tablespoons smooth white miso paste

8 ounces firm or soft tofu, cut into ½-inch cubes

Handful of finely minced scallions, chives, or pale green leek tops

Cooked sushi rice, to serve (optional)

Ume plum paste, to serve (optional)

1   Dice the cooked kombu into thin strips, about 1 × ¼ inch. Reserve ½ cup of the dashi in a mug or spouted cup, and heat the rest over medium heat with the minced kombu and the wakame. Once the wakame is thoroughly soft, about 8 minutes, turn off the heat.

2   Thin the miso paste by mixing it with the reserved dashi, then stir the mixture into the pot. Taste to establish that you have added

recipe continues

enough miso and adjust as needed. Gently stir in the tofu cubes and scallions. If you are feeding my son or anyone ready for quiet solids after a stretch of complaint, serve this with a bowl of rice on the side, and a dollop of ume plum paste. Aahhh. That's better.

DASHI

Dashi is a savory, umami-laden broth that is the main reason miso soup in a restaurant tastes different from miso soup you make at home. It's a nutrient-rich broth that is an excellent restorative on its own. It is also simple to prepare and takes well to fiddling (see variations after the recipe).

ABOUT 4 CUPS

4-inch piece dried kombu seaweed

4 cups water

1 cup loosely packed dried bonito flakes (katsuobushi)

1   Add the kombu and water to a medium saucepan and soak for 20 minutes.

2   Warm the water and kombu over medium-low heat. Never letting it rise above a low simmer, cook for at least 5 minutes and up to 30. *Never let it boil.* Got that? Low heat. No boiling, or the taste will be funny.

3   Remove the kombu, slice it thinly, and set it aside; you will add it to the soup.

4   Add the bonito flakes to the pot and turn off the heat. Let it stand 1 minute.

5 Strain the flakes from the broth and discard them. The broth can be used immediately, refrigerated for up to a week, or frozen for up to 3 months.

6 Bring the strained basic dashi to a simmer over medium-high heat. Turn off the heat and add the chosen ingredients. Cover the pot to allow the aromatics to steep, about 5 minutes. Strain again through the same fine-mesh sieve, pressing the solids gently to encourage all the liquid to drain.

OTHER WAYS TO DO IT

To make enhanced dashi, prepare any or all of the following:

- A FEW THIN SLICES OF LEMON, LIME, OR ORANGE

- A SMALL HANDFUL OF FRESH, BRIGHT GREENS, SUCH AS CILANTRO, PARSLEY, OR BABY SPINACH

- 1 SCALLION OR THE TENDER INNER PARTS OF A LEEK, CHOPPED

- 1 TEASPOON GRATED FRESH GINGER AND/OR TURMERIC ROOT

- 1–2 DRIED SHIITAKE MUSHROOMS

VEGETABLE BROTH

I was a vegetarian for twenty-odd years and in that time I tasted a lot of vegetable broth. I can report that in the main, it is a dull, miserable business. Packaged vegetable broth in particular is a misery, usually too sweet or too salty, cabbage-y tasting, or otherwise reminiscent of dishwater. I would rather use plain water. For an ailing person who does not do business with chicken broth, however, you need a tasty vegetable broth.

MAKES 8 CUPS

2 tablespoons uncooked white rice

One 2- to 3-inch knob fresh ginger root, peeled with a teaspoon and halved lengthwise

1 large leek, tough ends cut away, halved lengthwise and cleaned

1 small firm-ripe tomato, halved

10 cups water

2 ounces mushroom stems (from about 8 ounces mushrooms), or 4 dried shiitakes

1 head of garlic, intact, cut in half horizontally

1 stalk lemongrass, dry top end trimmed and discarded, bulb end

smashed with the side of a knife

One 1 × 2-inch ribbon lemon zest, removed with a vegetable peeler

1 teaspoon whole black peppercorns

1 teaspoon sugar

1–2 tablespoons tamari or soy sauce, or 1–2 teaspoons sea salt

1   Have a stock pot ready to accept the broth flavorings as you prepare them.

2   Toast the rice over medium heat in a small heavy skillet for about a minute, until lightly colored and fragrant; remove to the waiting pot.

3 In the same skillet, one at a time, scorch the ginger, then the leek, then the tomato. Turn the pieces until they are scorched black in places on all sides, a few minutes each. Add them all to the pot.

4 Add the water, the mushrooms, garlic, lemongrass, lemon zest, peppercorns, and sugar to the pot and bring to a high simmer. Reduce the heat to low, cover, and simmer for 45 minutes. Strain through a fine-mesh sieve or cheesecloth-lined strainer. Add the tamari. Taste and adjust; salt for punch, sugar (in tiny amounts) for balance and body.

5 The broth can be used immediately, refrigerated for up to a week, or frozen for up to 3 months.

Chicken Essence

The world hardly needs another recipe for chicken stock or bone broth, hip item that it has become—though if you need good instructions on how to create it, I recommend Michael Ruhlman or Jennifer McGruther as your guides. For centuries, on all points of the compass, mothers and nursemaids have had a more heavy-duty weapon up their sleeves: chicken essence. In place of the volumes of water that stock begins with, this method adds no liquid at all, extracting a rich, full-bodied broth that is a go-to restorative for exam time, new-mom time, and any other period of demand or recovery. Even science says it works. In Chinatowns everywhere, you can buy a special pot to make this in that has a funnel for steam, but it's easy to rig up something simple with equipment that you likely already have in your kitchen.

MAKES ABOUT 2 CUPS

2 pounds chicken wings

3–5 dried shiitake mushrooms

3–4 scallions, white and light green parts only, cleaned and cut into 2-inch sections

3 slices fresh ginger root, about ¼-inch thick

3 teaspoons Chinese cooking wine or any dry white wine

1   Ask the butcher to whack the chicken wings into three pieces for you, if you do not have a big sharp cleaver and/or do not want to deal with this task on your own. Make sure you get the wing tips (usually discarded by markets) as well as the two meatier sections.

2   Gather your cooking tools. You will need:

- 3 QUART-SIZE MASON JARS
- A LARGE POT WITH A SNUG COVER, TALL ENOUGH TO ACCOMMODATE THE MASON JARS
- A RACK OR SILICONE TRIVET THAT FITS INTO THE BASE OF THE POT
- A KETTLE OF HOT WATER

3 Divide the chicken pieces, aromatics (mushrooms, scallions, and ginger), and wine among the three jars—it's okay if they are pretty full—and set the uncovered jars into the pot. Add tap water to the pot, to come halfway up the sides of the jars, then cover the pot and set it over high heat until the water comes to a boil.

4 Reduce the heat to a strong simmer; allow to cook, covered snugly, for 3 hours, checking periodically to make sure there is ample water around the jars in the pot. If you need to replenish it, use water you have heated in the kettle, as adding water straight from the tap is likely to crack the jars.

5 After three hours, each jar should contain utterly exhausted bones and meat, as well as broth to about halfway up each of the jars. Strain the broth through a fine sieve.

6 Refrigerate the broth for at least a few hours or overnight. The broth part will solidify to a remarkably firm mass, allowing you to skim the fat (an excellent cooking medium, should you be planning to sauté anything). A quick reheat over a low flame will re-melt the broth, of which about ½ cup is an ample portion. It's quite savory and really needs nothing, but a pinch of salt or light squeeze of lemon does brighten the flavors a bit.

7 The broth can be refrigerated for up to a week or frozen for up to 3 months.

Two Levels of Rice Soup

This soup is adaptable to a range of needs and appetites. At level one, a simple rice broth is given just a hint of flavor from fennel seed (or substitute cumin seed; both are considered digestives); this is about as soothing and easy as food can be. At level two, vegetables are added to give a little more substance.

MAKES 4 CUPS

For the RICE BROTH (LEVEL ONE)

½ cup white rice

6 cups water

½ teaspoon salt

¼ teaspoon fennel or cumin seeds

For the GENTLEST SOUP (LEVEL TWO)

4–8 cloves of garlic (about 1 ounce)

1 medium-size fennel bulb, tough outer layer removed

(10–12 ounces), cleaned

2 big handfuls (about 2 ounces) baby spinach, chopped (optional)

½ teaspoon finely grated lemon zest

1 Combine the rice and water in a medium saucepan and bring to a boil. Lower the heat to a simmer and cook for 10 minutes. Let stand, covered, for another 10 minutes, stirring occasionally. Strain the liquid through a fine-mesh sieve set over a bowl, discard (or eat, or gift to the dog) the solids, and return the broth to the pot. Add the salt and fennel seeds and return to a simmer; cook for an additional 3–5 minutes, strain. Serve this simple rice broth warm.

2 To proceed to level two, peel the garlic cloves but leave them whole. Chop the fennel into ½-inch dice (you should have about 2 cups).

3 Add the fennel and garlic to the broth pot and bring to a simmer. Cook for about 30 minutes, until the vegetables are quiet tender. Remove from the heat.

4 If you are including the spinach, drop it in at this point and let it cook in the soup's residual heat for about 1 minute.

5 Using an immersion blender, or working in batches in a regular one, puree the soup until quite smooth.

6 You can strain the soup through a coarse mesh strainer to catch any fennel fibers or spinach leaves that have escaped the blades, but this is optional (and unnecessary, if you have a powerful blender).

7 Add the lemon zest and adjust for salt.

8 The broth or soup can be used immediately, refrigerated for up to 3 days, or frozen for up to 3 months.

TWO-LAYER KANTEN

Sickroom food can and should, at least some of the time, be pretty; pleasure and appetite are connected and run their wires through every one of our senses. Kanten is a Japanese dessert, one that brings the jiggly satisfaction of gelatin to the table with a little bit more nutritional candlepower. There are as many ways to make it as there are fruits under the sun. I set it up here with papaya, which has wonderful tummy-soothing properties, and guanabana (also known as soursop) juice, which is exotic to most of us but readily available canned or packed in aseptic packs in most Latin sections of big markets. Guanabana has a lot of history as a digestion-soother, blood-builder, and nerve-calmer, so paired with the papaya it makes a pretty soothing concoction. The bottom layer, with its double thickeners, is pudding-ish in consistency, while the top is more of a jiggly gelatin situation; either can easily stand alone. These fruits are one of a zillion possible options; mix up the juices to suit what sounds good and what you have near to hand (see notes following the recipe for a few suggestions.) I prefer agar in powder form for its ease of use, but flakes work just as well. Kuzu, a Japanese starch sold near the seaweeds and other like items in many groceries, is interchangeable with its more commonly available American cousin, arrowroot.

SERVES 8

For the
BOTTOM LAYER
¾ teaspoon agar powder or 2¼ teaspoons agar flakes

1 cup papaya or mango puree

½ cup water

2 tablespoons honey or agave syrup

Scrape of finely grated orange or lime zest

2 teaspoons kuzu or arrowroot powder

¼ cup water

For the
TOP LAYER
1 cup guanabana juice (see headnote)

¼ teaspoon agar powder or ¾ teaspoon agar flakes

1 tablespoon honey or agave syrup

To
SERVE
Pomegranate arils or fresh mint (optional)

1   Have ready a two-cup glass measuring cup and about eight little clear glasses (shot or sherry glasses are nice), at least 2 inches deep.

2   Prepare the bottom layer. Combine the agar, papaya puree, water, honey, and zest in a medium saucepan and whisk well to combine. Bring to a simmer over low to medium heat, and cook, stirring, for 3 minutes. If you're using agar flakes, they should be mostly dissolved at this point.

3   Combine the kuzu and water in a small cup or bowl and mix until smooth. Slowly dribble this slurry into the hot agar mixture, stirring all the while.

4   Continue to heat, stirring, for another 3 minutes, until it begins to thicken.

5   Portion this mixture among the waiting dishes and allow to fully cool to room temperature. As it cools, prepare the top layer.

6   Combine the juice with the agar and agave in a small saucepan and stir well. Bring to a simmer over low to medium heat, and cook, stirring, for 3–5 minutes, until slightly thickened.

7   Pour the mixture into the two-cup measure and allow it to stand at room temperature, stirring every few minutes, for 5–10 minutes, until it is no longer too hot to touch.

8   Gently pour the mixture onto the set fruit puree in the little glasses, and allow to fully cool at room temperature before refrigerating.

recipe continues

9 A little scattering of pomegranate arils or some bright, fresh mint makes this look especially fancy and cheering.

OTHER WAYS TO DO IT

It's nice to get some contrast between the layers—denser and more fruity on the bottom, and creamy or clear on the top.

- FOR THE BOTTOM LAYER, TRY PEACH PUREE; A COMMERCIALLY AVAILABLE MANGO SMOOTHIE, SUCH AS ODWALLA'S MANGO TANGO, OFFERS A QUICK AND TASTY SOLUTION.

- FOR THE TOP LAYER, CONSIDER PLANT MILKS, ALOE JUICE, OR COCONUT WATER. YOU CAN ALSO USE AN HERBAL TEA (MINT OR VERBENA ARE NICE) IN PLACE OF JUICE; THE LITTLE HIT OF AROMATIC FLAVOR IS A NICE SURPRISE AND AN EXCEPTIONALLY DIGESTIBLE OPTION.

ANGEL REMEDY

My dad is not very oriented toward the outdoors or DIY projects, but about forty years ago he started planting fruit trees, and among the torrent of produce that emerges from his orchard are astonishing numbers of Asian pears. Many people call these fruits "apple pears" due to their apple shape and texture. When my children were tots and prone to malaprops, one of them garbled the name into "angel apples." I cast around wildly for ways to use them up because they are not suited to juicing, jamming, or dehydrating. It turns out they are much revered in Korea as a throat remedy; Korean mamas do a special thing to them with ginger and steaming that inspires a lot of Internet odes. This potion engages ginger, lemon, and honey with the raw fruit, and during a bout of bronchitis one winter I was pretty tempted to pen an ode of my own. If you're in the wrong season or zip code for Asian pears, substitute any fruit near to hand; you can make it with a crisp apple and/or pear, or with oranges and cranberries, and I've made gorgeous versions in summer with fresh currants and gooseberries, or firm, ripe stone fruits like peaches and plums. People in robust health can just enjoy it in soda water over ice.

MAKES ABOUT 4 CUPS

1 medium or 2 small organic lemons
Juice of 2–4 lemons (about ½ cup to start, and you may want a little more)

One 2-inch knob fresh ginger root
One 1-inch knob fresh turmeric root (optional)
1–2 fresh Asian pears (about 12 ounces)

1 fresh hot red chili, or 2–3 teaspoons crushed red pepper flakes
½–1 cup high-quality raw honey

1 With a small sharp knife, score the rind of the organic lemon(s) all over to open some of the oil-holding cells. Using a larger sharp knife, quarter the lemon lengthwise into wedges, and then cut the wedges crosswise into very thin slices. If you want to get fussy, flick the seeds

recipe continues

out of these slices and discard them. Put the lemon slices in a medium bowl and add the lemon juice.

2   Using an ordinary teaspoon, peel the ginger (and the turmeric, if using) of its thin papery peel, which tends to be bitter. Slice the peeled root crosswise into very thin coins, then stack the coins four or five deep and cut them into extremely thin matchsticks. Add these to the lemons.

3   Cut the fruit into quarters (no need to peel), core, and then cut into eighths. Slice these very thinly crosswise, as you did the lemons, and toss them in the bowl.

4   Using commonsense precautions (gloves, or just extra care not to touch your eyeball later), cut the chili into little bits. If you are nervous, discard the seeds. If you are highly tolerant of heat or desperate for relief, then keep them. (I keep them.) Add the chili to the bowl.

5   Pour about ½ cup of the honey over the mixture and mix well. Let it stand on the counter for a few hours, macerating away while you shuffle around doing other things. A surprising amount of juice should accumulate. Stir and taste the mixture (taking care not to double dip); add as much of the remaining ½ cup honey as you like, and/or more lemon juice to create a satisfying, strong balance of tart and sweet. Pour it, solids and all, into a clean jar with a tight-fitting, corrosion-proof lid. Tuck it into the fridge.

6   When circumstances demand it, spoon a heaping glop of the fruit and liquid into a mug, bash them up a little with the spoon, and top with very hot water. A travel mug is nice because the lid strains things as you drink and also makes it ten times less likely you will spill it in

the bedclothes. In the event of a coughing fit, a spoonful of the nectar, neat, is a gift from the angels.

7   This potion keeps for weeks in the fridge, since both honey and lemon are natural preservatives, but in my house it is usually long gone before its storage limits have been tested.

GARLIC LEMONADE

It sounds like a practical joke but in fact garlic lemonade is an enchanted potion, introduced to me via a very beautiful garlic farmer named Jen who is such a compelling human that she could tell me to rub dirt in my ears and I would absolutely do it without waiting to hear what it might cure me of. Garlic lemonade is just as good for healthy people who aren't even thinking about germs (which is a pretty quick route to catching some) as it is for people who are sick or feel threatened by sickness. Regardless, in all likelihood it will be the desperate snork of a sinus issue or the repeated hornk of a lingering cough that will drive you to discover how appealing this strange concoction is. You don't have to include the ginger but if you must repeatedly remind yourself that no one ever died of a common cold, you probably should. Ginger's cousin, turmeric, is a worthy addition if a super-sore throat or other inflammation is part of the picture. Both also happen to taste delicious!

MAKES 8 CUPS

8 cups water	One 1-inch knob fresh	Juice of 1–2 lemons
8–10 cloves garlic, whole	ginger, peeled and	(about ¼ cup)
and peeled	chopped, or fresh	¼ cup honey
	turmeric (optional)	

1 Combine the water and the garlic (and ginger, if using) in a medium pot. Bring to a boil, then lower the heat, cover, and simmer for 1 hour.

2 Remove from the heat and pour the mixture through a fine-mesh strainer (do not press the solids; simply let them drain and then discard them). Add the lemon juice and the honey. Take it hot, or refrigerate and serve it over tons of ice. Feel better soon. The lemonade can be kept, refrigerated, for up to 1 week.

RECOVERY

In recovery, what someone is hungry for and drawn to are important factors; the person in question is rebuilding depleted stores of energy and who knows what else. Though more substantial than straight-up sickroom food, I still like to keep foods simple so their main quality—savory, cool, warming, slippery— is obvious to the recipient.

CHAWANMUSHI

This Japanese savory custard brings protein, minerals, and flavor back to the plate in their gentlest form. Delicious warm or chilled, and endlessly variable with the addition of vegetables and other niblets as appetite and constitution dictate, it makes a welcome switch from the sweets that tend to dominate the sickroom tray. With the optional add-ons, the custards become a nice addition to a light meal for regular, recovered people.

SERVES 4

For the
CUSTARD

1 teaspoon mirin or sake

1 teaspoon tamari or soy sauce

3 eggs

2 cups Dashi, cooled (see page 86) or broth

To
SERVE

Tamari or soy sauce

Sesame oil

Fresh herbs like parsley, cilantro, or dill; tender leaves only, minced (optional)

White or black sesame seeds (optional)

Dulse or nori flakes (optional)

1 Prepare a steamer rack: set a rack or vegetable steamer in a large pan so that it provides a level surface about 2 inches above some simmering water. Get four 6-ounce ramekins out and cut foil squares to cover them. Have a fine-mesh strainer near to hand.

2 In a medium bowl, whisk the mirin and tamari with the eggs, then whisk in the dashi.

3 Divide the custard among the ramekins by pouring it through the strainer. Cover each ramekin snugly with foil, and set them on the rack in your steamer pot. Steam for 10 minutes (no longer). Remove the ramekins from the steamer to a rack to cool slightly before serving warm, or cool completely in order to chill and serve cold.

4   Garnish before serving with tiny drizzles of tamari and sesame oil, and a sprinkling of any or all of the garnishes suggested.

OTHER WAYS TO DO IT

To take these custards to the next level, the one where light meals are served at tables, consider these possibilities to divide among the tops:

- ABOUT 1 CUP OF TINY CUBES OF SWEET POTATO, DICED ASPARAGUS, OR FINELY SLICED GREEN BEANS, STEAMED UNTIL TENDER

- ABOUT ½ CUP OF SHREDDED COOKED CHICKEN, TINY CUBES OF SEASONED TOFU, FLAKES OF BAKED OR SMOKED SALMON OR TROUT, OR CRISPED AND CRUMBLED BACON

- A SCALLION, WHITE AND LIGHT GREEN PARTS, FINELY MINCED AND QUICKLY SAUTÉED IN NEUTRAL OIL (OR THE FAT RENDERED FROM THE BACON)

- 1 TABLESPOON OF MINCED FRESH BASIL

CONGEE

If you are lucky enough to be loved by Millie Chan, as I have been my whole life, you may have received a container of congee, also known as juk, when your spirit or body was overwhelmed. I have seen a lot of pots of congee pass from her kitchen into my family's kitchens, and when asked to make a meal of exceptional gentleness and appeal for a friend in need, this is my first thought. The process could hardly be simpler. Enormous reward-to-effort ratio makes it even more satisfying. You can make it with any kind or combination of rice, or (my favorite variation) a fifty-fifty blend of rice and millet, or any whole grains. You're just taking the trifecta of messed-up rice cookery (using too much water, stirring, and overcooking), and owning it.

Congee can be made with water and also with stock or broth. Its grainy simplicity is a nice ramp-up to recovery from any blow—emotional, physical, or digestive. If you tuck some roasted squash or garlicky greens into the basket, along with some peppy condiments, every member of the receiving line can make it how they like it.

SERVES 6, OR MAKES 8 CUPS

1 cup short-grain brown rice or other whole grains (see headnote)

10 cups water (or a mixture of water and broth)

1 teaspoon kosher salt

For
CHICKEN OR FISH CONGEE (OPTIONAL)

1 whole boneless chicken breast, or
½ pound mild white fish

2 teaspoons cornstarch (if using chicken; omit for fish)

1 teaspoon salt

Freshly ground pepper

½ teaspoon sesame oil

To
SERVE

Finely minced fresh ginger

Coarsely chopped fresh cilantro

Minced scallions

Sesame oil

Tamari or soy sauce

Hot sauce

1   Combine the rice and water in a large heavy pot. Bring to a boil, stir quite thoroughly, then turn the heat as low as it will go and simmer gently, covered, for 1½ hours. Really. Stir occasionally, at closer intervals at the start of cooking, to keep the grains suspended, and as you near the end of cooking to make sure the porridge doesn't scorch on the bottom once it begins to thicken.

2   When the congee is done, it will look like a thick, smooth gruel with barely visible rice kernels (think oatmeal), and if you've never tried it, you will wonder what in the world I am having you do. Stir in the salt. Now you have plain congee, and you can stop there and go straight for the garnish.

3   If you want chicken congee, then while the rice is simmering, finely sliver the chicken breast (using a very sharp knife and a partially frozen piece of chicken will simplify this task immeasurably). Don't try to make it perfect, just chop it tiny as best you can. Toss the chicken in a small bowl with the cornstarch, salt, a few grinds of pepper, and sesame oil. The attempt to toss will lead to a worrisome clump, but mix as well as possible and it will work out fine in the end. When the congee is done, take it off the heat, stir the seasoned chicken into the pot, and keep stirring to separate the chicken pieces, until the chicken meat turns white. It will cook in a jiffy in the heat of the hot porridge.

4   If you are making fish congee, season the raw fish with the salt, a few grinds of pepper, and the sesame oil. Portion the fish among the bowls and ladle the hot rice over it. This will cook the fish.

5   Garnish bowls of congee with a sprinkle of ginger, cilantro, and scallions, a light drizzle each of sesame oil and soy sauce, and if you are feeling the need for some heat, a little kick of hot sauce.

AGUADITO, A RICHLY GREEN SOUP

I have only good things to say about plain chicken soup. It is the basic currency of caretaking and people tend to respond to it like dogs to a bell, with an inner voice announcing "I am being looked after!" Aguadito is a souped-up version from Peru, pungent with herbs and tangy with lime and carrying a little bit of heat, which all seems to add up to just the right thing for a dense head cold, or other complaints that cry out for a little ba-da-bing to make them right. You can swap out the chicken stock for Vegetable Broth (page 88) and use tofu in place of the chicken, if your target audience is not made up of omnivores.

SERVES 4 TO 6

For
CHICKEN SOUP
8 cups chicken stock
1½ pounds bone-in
   chicken breast

For
VEGETARIAN SOUP
8 cups vegetable stock
One 15-ounce block
   firm tofu, frozen
   overnight and thawed

For
BOTH SOUPS
1 medium yellow onion,
   finely chopped

3 cloves garlic, peeled
   but whole, divided
3–5 dried whole red
   bird chilies
½ cup mild lager or ale
   (optional)
One 1- to 2-inch knob
   fresh ginger root,
   chopped or grated
1 bunch fresh cilantro
   or dill
Salt and freshly ground
   pepper
Pinch of cayenne
   pepper
Zest of ½ lime, finely
   grated

Juice of ½ lime (about
   1 tablespoon); reserve
   the remaining ½ lime
   in wedges, to serve
1 tablespoon olive oil
2 big handfuls (about
   2 ounces) baby
   spinach leaves
¼ cup water
¾ cup long-grain rice
Salt
1 cup corn kernels
   (optional)

1 Heat the stock in a large saucepan with the onion, two cloves of the garlic, the chilies, beer, if using, and ginger. Remove the cilantro leaves from the stems. Set the leaves aside and add the stems to the broth. Bring to a simmer as you prepare the other items.

2 To prepare the chicken, preheat the oven to 375°F (you will be baking the chicken immediately after broiling it). Season the chicken with salt, pepper, cayenne, lime zest, lime juice, and olive oil. Switch the oven to broil and broil the meat about 8 minutes, until golden brown, then bake it for about 25 minutes, until cooked through (to an internal temperature of 165°). Pull the chicken from the bone, shredding it. Add the bones and skin, as well as any juices that accumulated in the pan when you cooked it, to the broth pot, and leave that to simmer while you continue your preparations.

3 To prepare the tofu, shred or coarsely grate it, then set it on a few stacks of paper towel to drain. Season these with salt, pepper, cayenne, lime zest, and lime juice. Heat the olive oil in a small skillet, and sauté for about 7 minutes, until light golden. Set aside.

4 In a blender, combine the cilantro leaves, spinach, the remaining clove of garlic, and the water; blend until smooth.

5 Strain the broth (discarding the solids).

6 Add the cilantro slurry to the broth, along with the shredded chicken or tofu. Add the rice and corn, if using, and bring to a simmer. Continue cooking for about 20 minutes, until the rice is cooked. Serve with wedges of lime.

7 This soup can be used immediately, refrigerated for up to 3 days, or frozen for up to 3 months.

SLIPPERY SOUP

If fancy royal visitors are coming in their carriage to dine, don't make this. This soup is for restoration, rehydration, and recovery, not dinner parties. You don't have to tell me it's slippery because that's the whole point of it, to soothe parched throats and rehydrate systems with an almost unctuous, savory balm. If it's what a person needs, it will hit the spot.

SERVES 2

½ cup dry navy beans or other tiny white beans, soaked overnight in water to cover with a pinch of baking soda

6 cups water

1–2 strips dried kombu seaweed

1 large carrot, cut into 2-inch chunks

¼ cup sweet brown rice or pearled barley (if gluten is not an issue)

2–4 cloves garlic, peeled but whole

2 tablespoons whole flax seeds

1 teaspoon smooth white miso paste or salt

Lemon wedge, to serve

Optional Additions,
TO SERVE
The reserved navy beans

1 small yam, peeled and finely diced

1 Drain and rinse the beans. In a small saucepan, cover the beans with the water and bring to a simmer. Cook the beans, covered, until just tender, a time which will vary by the unknowable factor of the age of the beans; plan on 45 minutes and test as you go. Strain the liquid over a bowl, reserving the beans. Return the liquid to the pot.

2 Add the kombu, carrots, rice, garlic, and flax seeds to the bean broth. Simmer for about 35 minutes, until the carrots are very tender and rice is entirely cooked. Strain the broth through a fine strainer and season it with the miso.

3   Now you have some options, depending on whether your quarry here is up for solids. You can serve the broth alone, or you can draw the kombu out of the strainer, chop it up fine, and add it back to the pot with the carrot, chopped, and the yam, if using, as well as the reserved beans. Cook for about 10 minutes, just until the yam is tender.

4   Either way, broth or chunky soup, add a squeeze of lemon before serving.

5   This soup can be served immediately, or refrigerated for up to 3 days.

GINGER CUSTARD

This simple pudding has its roots in Chinese cuisine (and Chinese medicine, where ginger is considered an essential warming and digestive agent), and is basically magic. I know there is a perfectly plausible scientific explanation for what takes place here because the interwebs are full of people who have nerded out on the principles at work. I've attended to the factors they identified here, but I still think it is actually magic that produces this gentle custard, with a silky texture that is all comfort and packs a warming, gingery kick.

I like to make it in teacups but any small bowl will do. Use beige and papery-skinned mature ginger (not younger spring ginger, which is pinkish white), and do not prepare the ginger juice more than a few minutes before you plan to use it, or the fairies will not oblige you (it has something to do with enzymes, if you must know). I have found that a ½ teaspoon of ginger juice per serving is the minimum amount required to make the pudding set; you can definitely use more, up to 1 teaspoon per serving—some tasters craved more ginger and others balked at a hint of bitterness when the proportions climbed.

SERVES 2

One 1-inch knob fresh ginger root	1 cup pasteurized whole milk (raw milk will not set)	2 teaspoons sugar or honey

1 Have two small (4- to 6-ounce capacity) bowls at the ready, and two small plates or saucers to cover them.

2 Using a Microplane grater, grate the ginger and squeeze out the juice (I use my hands). Peeling the ginger (use an ordinary teaspoon) makes the flavor a little milder. You need 1 teaspoon total. Divide the ginger juice between the two bowls. Do not do this ahead; do it immediately before you heat the milk.

3   Combine the milk and sugar in a small pan and heat carefully over low heat, stirring to dissolve the sweetener, to 150°F. If you do not have a thermometer, watch for a tiny bubble at the edge of the pan to indicate you should turn off the heat; 150°F is warm to the finger, edging toward uncomfortable if you keep it in there for about 20 seconds.

4   Pour the warmed milk into the ginger juice in each cup from a height of a few inches, so that the pouring creates a thorough mixing of the two liquids. Do not stir. Cover with the saucers and leave to set at room temperature. It should be set after 5–10 minutes. The custard may be served immediately, warm, or chilled in the fridge. It's best on the day it is made, but will keep for about 2 days.

INTERNATIONALLY KNOWN RICE PUDDING

There's more that connects us than divides us, across the globe, than the headlines might let on. To wit: there is a Cypriot dish, a simple rice flour pudding, known as muhalebbi, *which is so, so similar to an Israeli pudding known as* malabi. *A Lebanese rice flour pudding known as* meghli *is traditionally served to pregnant women to help them grow strong babies, and in Puerto Rico, a pudding known as* majarete *made with either rice or corn accomplishes a similar purpose.* Shalom aleichem, Salaam alaikum, *peace be with you. Some of these rice puddings are enriched with copious amounts of spices, some use brown sugar and others white. They are all an eggless custard, milk fortified with a little grain to make a digestible and soothing offering suitable for the recovering as well as the upright. It may not be your mother's rice pudding, but it surely is someone's mother's, and it's a smooth, lovely alternative to the gritty or grainy rice puddings that you might be citing as the foundation of your resistance to rice puddings in general. Note that sweet rice flour will not work here; you want regular rice flour, of the type sold in bulk bins. Brown or white work equally well.*

SERVES 6 TO 8

4 cups carton-type coconut milk or cow's milk (or a blend of the two), divided

½ cup white or brown rice flour

¼ cup sugar or honey

½ teaspoon sea salt

½ teaspoon rosewater, orange blossom water, or vanilla extract

Plum or peach jam, roasted fruit, or fresh berries, to serve

1 Measure 3½ cups of the milk into a medium saucepan and heat over medium heat to almost boiling point.

2 Mix the flour with the remaining ½ cup milk in a heatproof cup, stirring until smooth.

3 Slowly pour about one-third of the hot milk into the flour paste, stirring well.

4 Return the mixture to the milk in the saucepan and stir very well to combine. Cook over gentle heat while whisking continuously for about 5–8 minutes, until the mixture is thickened. Add the sugar and salt, and continue to cook and whisk until the whisk leaves visible streaks, another 5–7 minutes. Take off the heat and stir in the rosewater or vanilla.

5 To enhance the texture, stir the pudding for about 10 minutes as it cools, a process you can hasten by decanting it into a mixing bowl and even immersing the bowl in a larger container of ice water. Pour the cooled mixture into 6–8 small bowls. If you'd like to prevent a skin from forming at the top, very lightly butter some parchment paper circles and press these over the surface of the puddings.

6 Cool to room temperature and then chill thoroughly (about 2 hours) before eating.

7 Serve with a dollop of jam, roasted fruit, or fresh berries.

WELLNESS TRUFFLES

When I was pregnant with my first child, I worked at an art school in a rural neighborhood. When the lovely woman who lived next door to the school heard I was expecting a baby, she offered her spare room "in case I felt sleepy and needed a nap." A nap! Ha. I was much too grown up and busy for naps. I made some polite response. About three weeks later, I was sitting at my desk and noticed that my body, especially around the eyelid area, seemed to be made entirely of concrete. I dragged myself the hundred yards to Jane's house and collapsed into her guest bed. A master gardener and herbalist, a loving parent and an incredible cook, over the years of my family's infancy she more than taught me how to do things, she taught me how I wanted to do The Whole Thing. When she caught me hanging on her every herbal word, Jane gave me a copy of a terrific primer called Ten Essential Herbs by Lalitha Thomas, and there I learned to respect the gentle balancing powers of slippery elm, which can both—shall we say—get train service restored on a stopped digestive tract and also slow down the express. These little mouthfuls are a good vehicle for taking it in; sweet and tangy and with none of the gloop factor that mixing it in water is known for. You'll want to bring them on a tray with a big glass of water though, because that's this herb's best ally.

MAKES ABOUT 8 TRUFFLES

For the
BASE

2 tablespoons raw honey

2 tablespoons melted unrefined coconut oil

¼ teaspoon vanilla extract

1 tablespoon lemon juice

Zest of 1 lemon, finely grated

2 teaspoons finely grated fresh ginger, or 1 teaspoon ground ginger

For a
NEUTRAL, BALANCING EFFECT

⅓ cup (25g) slippery elm powder

To
MOVE THINGS ALONG A LITTLE

3 tablespoons (12g) slippery elm powder

2 tablespoons (12g) golden flax meal

1 tablespoon (3g) psyllium husk powder

1   Prepare the base. In a small bowl, cream the honey and oil together well. Beat in the vanilla, lemon juice, lemon zest, and ginger.

2   Combine the herbs of your choice with the honey mixture. The mixture will appear soft until the coconut oil cools down completely. Refrigerate or leave at a cool room temperature until firm. Use a small spoon and your palms to roll the herbal mixture into marble-size portions, and store these in a tightly covered container in the refrigerator for up to a week. Because the herbs are so gentle, you don't need to worry about overeating these, as long as there's plenty of water to go along with them, but one or two is generally an elegant sufficiency.

OTHER WAYS TO DO IT

- SUBSTITUTE 2 TEASPOONS OF UNSWEETENED COCOA POWDER FOR AN EQUAL AMOUNT OF ANY OF THE OTHER DRY INGREDIENTS. IN THAT CASE, SWAP ORANGE JUICE AND ZEST FOR THE LEMON.

- ACCENTUATE THE TRUFFLE-ESQUE EFFECT BY ROLLING THE FINISHED BALLS IN COCONUT SHREDS, FLAX MEAL, FINELY CHOPPED NUTS, OR EVEN COCOA.

4

FOOD
FOR
SOLACE

WALK FEARLESSLY into the house of mourning, **FOR GRIEF IS ONLY LOVE** that has come up against its oldest challenge, and after all these mortal years, **LOVE KNOWS HOW TO HANDLE IT.**

KATE BRAESTRUP

I AM THE YOUNGEST OF THREE SISTERS. A FEW YEARS AGO, MY OLDEST SISTER DIED. THE TIME OF HER ILLNESS WAS TAXING FOR MANY REASONS, ONE OF WHICH WAS TRAVELING REQUIRED NEAR AND FAR TO HELP CARE FOR HER. THIS PERIOD FELT LIKE AN ENDLESS, FATHOMLESS EXPANSE OF PUSH AND PULL, OF NEVER QUITE BEING WHERE I WAS. MY MIND AND HEART WERE HALF AT HOME AND HALF WITH HER, WHICHEVER PLACE I HAPPENED, PHYSICALLY, TO BE. AND THEN IT ENDED, AS ILLUSIONS OF ENDLESSNESS OFTEN DO, AND WE TUMBLED, AS A FAMILY, INTO THE TRULY ENDLESS AND FATHOMLESS LANDSCAPE OF GRIEF.

I can't say that I had many conscious expectations about grief, having spent two years fervently hoping it would not be part of my near future. But I suppose, as I tumbled, I expected that the shift would be about the falling away of all the tasks and other distracting things mixed up in the tumult of her sickness and dying, about finding the pure sadness of loss. This was true, but it turned out to demand a great deal more time and labor than I imagined it would. Managing through an illness involves a lot of work, most of it not easy. But grief in the aftermath of one is not an exemption from labor. Grief is work: arduous, demanding, tiring *effort*, especially in its early stages.

Just about every moment of light in my life from the moment I received the first phone call about her diagnosis to the period after her death had light in it because of the goodness of friends. We were so thoroughly fed by the steel network of community around us that I lost count of my blessings. Already a big believer in the value of friends cooking for friends, I became essentially devout.

For months and months as I traveled and then as I faced the reality that I didn't need to travel any longer, friendship arrived at our doorstep as bags of bagels and baskets of fruit to fill my children's lunch boxes; as soups to freeze for later that tasted of an old friend's familiar hand in the kitchen and a new one's thunderclap of empathic feeling; as full gorgeous meals plunked right onto the table; and as the mailbox surprises of a bar of spicy Mexican hot chocolate, its sweetness carrying a welcome bite of heat, and a box of handpicked lemons sent from warmer climates to remind me that somewhere the sun was shining.

In the immediate aftermath of her death, someone who loves us got off a plane from a weeklong business trip and labored to make my family a *koliva*, a Greek food of mourning with pagan roots, traditionally eaten on the ninth day of grieving. Seeds, sweetness, and spices were beautifully arranged in the bowl she presented, adorned with blossoms though it was deep winter. The notion, she said, is to take in the seeds in the name of the departed. Once consumed, you carry on in the spirit of that person, whom you offer eternal life through your continued existence, I reckon, until someone eats a *koliva* for you, and on, and on.

It's impossible to overstate how essential all this was to our survival.

In case you have never been on the receiving end of this kind of support, and are worried your ministrations may be unwelcome or intrusive, let me just repeat that last bit again: it's impossible to overstate how welcome and sustaining and valuable your thoughtful offering can be when a person or a family is taxed in this way.

Positive psychologist and grief counselor Maria Sirois says that what is needed to support the grieving is the ability to "bear witness without flinching from darkness," and this feels like a tall order to some. Many people are alarmed and alienated by other people's grief, succumbing to a kind of paralysis in the face of it. Others don't want to intrude or bother, fearing that they might compound the stress of an already stressful time with unwanted intrusions.

It's so unlikely that your edible offering will be a bother. One beautifully liberating thing that I can testify to is that the scale of the delivery is unimportant. The bar of chocolate in an envelope, the bowl of hand-arranged seeds festooned with flowers, the homemade gingerbread people and the store-bought bagels, the pocket-sized gestures and the trunk-loads of food all made indelible impressions. Each one was a strand in the rope that tethered me to the land of the living and together they eventually pulled me to my feet again, altered but upright.

If you know the recipient well, it's likely you can think of something that will either save the day (like packed lunch boxes for their kids, or meals timed and constructed to the particular needs and tastes of their household) or simply remind them, gently, of pleasure at a time when pleasures are both scarce and suspect. If you don't know your recipients, use your own senses as a guide. Mine suggest that nothing so spicy as to be confronting (unless you know they crave it), nor too bland to be unappealing (since appetite may be low) should be offered. Food that isn't decadent, presented simply, and packed with sustenance, is just the thing for people who may not be remembering to eat.

Just showing up in this type of situation is the key, so let that free you from thoughts that you have to bake bread from wheat you thresh yourself. You can wing your way through the grocery store, pulling together a small collection of the items you think may appeal or be of use, and odds are that you will be on the mark. It's the fact that you are not flinching from their darkness that your recipients will be nourished by, and will remember.

As useful as it is in the immediate aftermath of loss, it's even more so a few weeks or months out, when the helpful hordes have thinned, and a person or a family confronts the expectation that mourning in some sense should be "over" even though it shows no sign of tapering off. Make contact right away with a grieving friend, so they know you are there, but don't feel rushed to make your offering.

Another thing I can attest to from both sides of the equation: grief is a situation that demands quite a bit more than food to navigate. Lots of things are said over and over by well-meaning people to their friends in need, especially after a death. Some of these rote phrases can actually transmit a great deal of meaning, depending on how they are said. "I'm sorry for your loss" has the capacity to convey both what we can sense and what we can't assume about another person's experience. That said, I have friends who detest it. It's all, I suppose, in the "who" and the "how" of the delivery. Again and again I hear grieving people struggle to accept that some friends have abandoned them in dark times, so here's a gentle urging to let go of the impulse to speak only when you have thought of the perfect thing to say. A friend who says, "I don't know what to say, but I'm here," offers a live connection; a friend who is mysteriously absent is an additional drain on a person who can ill afford more sorrow.

The phrase that chaps *me* is, "Please let me know if there's anything I can do." If you have ever found yourself at the bottom of one of life's deepest sand traps, then you know that it's pretty hard to identify your particular needs, and just about impossible to match a need you are aware of with one person in the sea of faces that may have offered general assistance.

Far more useful to an overwhelmed friend or acquaintance are offers like these, extended in the days and weeks of new grief (or, for that matter, new parenthood, or recovery of any kind):

- I'M CALLING YOU FROM THE GROCERY STORE/DRUGSTORE/OFFICE SUPPLY STORE AND DRIVING HOME RIGHT PAST YOUR HOUSE. IS THERE ANYTHING I CAN PICK UP FOR YOU? ARE YOU, FOR EXAMPLE, OUT OF TOILET PAPER OR SHAMPOO OR CAT FOOD?

- TOMORROW IS MY ERRAND DAY. CAN I GET/MAIL/RETURN ANYTHING IN MY TRAVELS AND SAVE YOU A TRIP? DO YOU NEED STAMPS OR YOUR DRY CLEANING ATTENDED TO?

- MY MORNING IS SUDDENLY OPEN AND I AM ITCHING TO GET OUTSIDE/GET MY HANDS DIRTY/ USE THIS CRAZY LOVE I HAVE OF SORTING MAIL AND FOLDING LAUNDRY! I'VE GOT TWO HOURS TO WALK YOUR DOG/WEED YOUR GARDEN/MAKE NEAT PILES OF ENVELOPES. HOW WOULD YOU LIKE ME TO USE THEM?

If the offer is *specific in nature, focused in time, and seems not to be causing you any extra trouble or travel*—almost doing you a favor—then those in need are much more likely to take you up on it. Use what you know how to do (you're a whiz at accounting, are known for your lovely handwriting, just got certified as a massage therapist), or just are plain willing to do (clean gutters, drive kids to school or the car to the mechanic) as one guide. Use what you know about the person as another, and shape your offer along those three guidelines. You'll almost always get a taker.

Utterly strapped for an idea? Within hours of a diagnosis or loss, a family's kitchen can become a windstorm of bagels and fruit trays, and tubs of hummus and cream cheese begin to replicate in the dark of the fridge. Roll up your sleeves, unflinching, and bring order to the fridge and counters. Slice excess bagels and freeze them, consolidate duplicate containers, remove furry things from the crisper, rearrange picked-over platters, take out the recycling and clean the sink and start a fresh pot of coffee and get rid, please, of the wilted flowers.

Here's the thing: No matter who has rushed to our side, pretty much every sad person ends up standing alone in the kitchen at some hour of the day or night. To see order there, to know that the prospect of wading through yet another task you'd rather not face has magically been lifted from your consciousness as if by well-meaning elves, well—that can be a huge gift.

BREAKFAST KOLIVA

A true koliva is a lot of work to create, as it is equal parts altarpiece and edible. They are beautiful, loving things to labor over and to present, and if you feel moved to build one, instructions abound on the interwebs as to their creation and backstory. The doctored-up oatmeal below borrows the poetry of the seeds and grains and fruits that my dear Andrea introduced to me and brings the ceremonial dish to the table as a nourishing breakfast. This is best when an overnight soak for the oats is part of the preparations, so plan ahead by a day if you can.

SERVES 4

1 cup steel-cut oats

½ teaspoon salt, divided

Scrape of finely grated orange zest

¼ teaspoon ground cinnamon

¼ cup dried cranberries

¼ cup chopped dried apricots

1 tablespoon sesame seeds

1 tablespoon hemp seeds

2 tablespoons sunflower seeds

¼ cup honey

To SERVE

Heavy cream or coconut cream

Sliced or slivered almonds, toasted

Arils of half a pomegranate

Honey

Unsalted butter or coconut oil

1   The night (or at least several hours) before you plan to serve this, put the oats in a pan with water to cover by 2 inches, along with ¼ teaspoon of salt. Bring to a boil, turn off the heat, and leave to cool, covered.

recipe continues

2   In the morning, cover with fresh water by a generous inch, adding the orange zest and cinnamon to the pot with the water. Stir well to incorporate, smoothing out any lumps. Bring this mixture to a boil, then lower the heat. Cook the oats at a low simmer for about 10 minutes, until the grains are quite tender and the mixture has thickened, stirring often to prevent sticking.

3   Add the cranberries, apricots, sesame seeds, hemp seeds, sunflower seeds, honey, and ¼ teaspoon of salt. Stir to combine, and let rest, covered, for a few minutes.

4   To serve immediately, portion into bowls, drizzle with a little cream, and sprinkle some almonds and pomegranate seeds and a drizzle of extra honey on top.

5   To tuck into a basket for someone to eat later, spread the mixture in a well-buttered 8 × 3-inch loaf pan or similar baking dish, or for single servings, into four buttered wide-mouth half-pint mason jars. Dot the surface(s) with butter or coconut oil and drizzle with honey. The pan can be heated, uncovered, in a 325°F oven; the jars should be set into a larger pan of hot water before heading into the oven. Make sure to include a small bottle of cream and teeny jars of pomegranate seeds and almonds in the basket, so the ceremony of drizzling and festooning can happen at serving time.

WILD RICE SOUP

This soup is full of flavors without being overwhelming, full of nutrition without being heavy, and a full meal in one bowl. There are many ways to tailor it to the tastes and preferences of your recipient. For the greens, you can use broccoli rabe, which admittedly is not to everyone's taste but I adore it, cleaned and chopped, or another sturdy green, like kale, which is more universally appealing. Whichever green you choose, reserve the other half-bunch for the Little Meatballs (page 127) or the UnMeatballs (page 129), which accompany the soup. Note that the rice should be soaked overnight in cold water to generously cover before making this soup.

SERVES 4 TO 6

3 tablespoons olive oil

1 medium yellow onion, diced (about 1½ cups)

1 teaspoon salt

1 medium leek, tough outer leaves removed, quartered, cleaned, and sliced fine

2 cloves garlic, minced

1 tablespoon ground cumin

2 teaspoons ground coriander

¼–½ teaspoon cayenne pepper

1–2 large carrots, peeled and diced (about 1 cup)

2–3 medium Yukon Gold or similar potatoes, peeled and diced (about 2 cups)

1 cup wild rice, soaked overnight and drained

8–10 cups vegetable or chicken broth

½ bunch broccoli rabe, kale, or other greens, stemmed and chopped (about 4 cups, loosely packed)

1 batch Little Meatballs (page 127) or UnMeatballs (page 129)

1   Heat the olive oil in a large pot over medium heat. Add the onion and the salt, and sauté for about 5 minutes, until it softens.

recipe continues

2   Add the leek and continue to sauté another 5 minutes, until both are lightly golden; add the garlic and sauté for 2 minutes more, keeping the heat low so the garlic does not brown.

3   Add the cumin, coriander, and cayenne to taste, and stir to release their fragrance; add the carrot and potatoes and stir to coat; add the drained rice and 8 cups of the broth. Bring to a simmer and leave there, for about 1 hour, covered, until the rice is sprung and tender. Keep an eye on the level of broth and add more, if needed, to keep things soupy. Keep the greens in reserve until serving time.

4   All of this will wait patiently now, until you are ready for it, and the soup will be the better for the waiting. When that time of readiness comes, you, or the recipient of your generosity, simply need to reheat the soup and drop in the greens. Separately heat the meatballs up, in the oven or in a skillet on the stove. When the greens are nicely cooked, about 7 minutes, taste the soup for seasoning (it should be pretty subtle, as the meatballs pack a wallop), and divide it among the bowls, dropping a little cluster of meatballs into each serving.

5   This soup can be used immediately, refrigerated for up to a week, or frozen for up to 3 months.

LITTLE MEATBALLS

These are super in the Wild Rice Soup (page 125), on top of pasta, or taken straight by the toothpick, fork, or weary hand—possibly dipped (see pages 132–33 for candidates), possibly neat. These meatballs represent all the nourishment needed to keep a weary person sustained in one tiny, savory package.

MAKES 50 TO 60 TINY MEATBALLS

½ bunch (about 8 ounces) sturdy greens, such as kale, broccoli rabe, or spinach, tough stems removed, leaves washed and dried

1 small to medium yellow onion (6–8 ounces)

1 pound ground chicken or any ground meat

3 tablespoons fresh breadcrumbs (I use a sturdy wheatless sandwich bread, like Sami's)

1 egg

2 tablespoons finely minced fresh parsley, basil, oregano, or thyme (or a mixture)

1½ teaspoons ground cumin

¾ teaspoon ground coriander

Pinch of cayenne pepper

¼ teaspoon ground turmeric

1½ teaspoons salt

Freshly ground pepper

About 3 tablespoons olive oil for frying

1   Very finely chop the greens; you should have about 2 cups. Separately, finely chop the onion. You can do this in a food processor with a series of pulses; just watch carefully that you don't puree them.

2   In a large bowl, mix the ground chicken with the minced greens, onions, breadcrumbs, egg, herbs, cumin, coriander, cayenne, turmeric, salt, and pepper until well combined. Cover and refrigerate for at least 10 minutes (and up to 1 hour), to allow the moisture in the ingredients to equalize.

recipe continues

3 Use a pair of teaspoons (or a tiny ice cream scoop—I love any excuse to use my tiny ice cream scoop) to form meatballs about the size of grapes or cherry tomatoes—as small as you can bear to fuss with, remembering that they will shrink a bit as they cook. I like to get at least fifty of them out of the mixture if I can maintain the necessary patience.

4 Heat 1 tablespoon of the oil in a heavy skillet set over medium heat until it ripples. Working in batches, cook the meatballs for about 7 minutes total, shaking the pan around so the little fellows get tossed and all sides get nice and toasty golden.

5 Remove each batch to a heatproof dish as they are done, to await their further deployment. Add more oil to the pan as needed. They can be held at room temperature for up to 4 hours, or (once cooled) refrigerated in a covered container for up to a week. You can also freeze the cooked meatballs for up to a month.

UNMEATBALLS

These adaptable little items come from a wonderful cookbook called Twelve Recipes *by Cal Peternell. They flex to accommodate both whole-grain and gluten-free bread, and the addition of some stealth pumpkin brings additional nourishment along with a very noshable texture. They work well with just about any green + herb combination. Like the Little Meatballs (page 127), these are delicious hot, room temperature, cold from the fridge at 3:00 a.m., eaten alone, plain or dipped in something wonderful (see Take a Dip, pages 132–33). They stand-in for meatballs over pasta, in the Wild Rice Soup (page 125), or on a stick. I generally require at least three reasons before I am willing to wash my food processor, and this recipe provides that: use it to pulse the bread, then the shallot, then the garlic and herbs, then the greens; fine mincing of all the components is the key to success here.*

MAKES 24 TO 30 TINY UNMEATBALLS

3 tablespoons olive oil

2 shallots, very finely minced (about ⅓ cup)

Salt and freshly ground pepper

2 cloves garlic, very finely minced (about 1 tablespoon)

½ cup finely minced fresh cilantro or parsley (or a combination)

1½ teaspoons cumin seeds

¼ teaspoon smoked paprika

½ bunch (about 8 ounces) sturdy greens, such as kale, chard, or spinach, tough stems removed, leaves washed and dried, very finely chopped

1½ cups fresh breadcrumbs

2 ounces (about ½ cup) crumbled feta

⅓ cup canned pure pumpkin puree

1 egg

2–3 tablespoons olive oil for frying

1 Heat a large skillet over medium-low heat and add the oil, shallots, and 1 teaspoon of salt. Cook, stirring occasionally, for about 6 minutes,

recipe continues

until soft and lightly browned. Add the garlic, herbs, cumin seeds, and paprika. Stir for 30 seconds.

2   Add the greens to the pan and sauté for 1–2 minutes, until they soften. Turn the mixture out into a medium mixing bowl.

3   Let cool for 5 minutes, then add the breadcrumbs, feta, and pumpkin. Mix well, then taste for seasoning. Add more salt and some pepper if necessary—this is your chance, while the mixture is egg-free, to taste and get the seasoning right.

4   Crack the egg into the bowl and mix it in very well.

5   Let the mixture rest in the fridge for 10–20 minutes, to regulate the moisture between the wet and binding ingredients and the breadcrumbs.

6   One scant tablespoon at a time, roll the mixture into balls. Once all the unmeatballs are formed, refrigerate the rolled balls for at least 30 minutes, to firm up a bit more.

7   Heat 2 tablespoons oil in a skillet over medium heat. Working in batches if necessary, add the balls to the pan—they should sizzle when they hit the oil—then turn heat down to medium-low (bread browns fast, so keep the heat on the lower side to keep these from burning). Use a small spoon to gently move them around, turning frequently. The mixture is soft, but the balls will hold together as soon as a cooked crust forms. Cook for about 8 minutes, until toasty brown on all sides.

8   Remove to a plate or heatproof dish. Serve immediately, hot or at room temperature, or cool and store to reheat later. They will keep for up to 1 week in the fridge. They can be frozen, wrapped securely, for up to a month.

STRONG TO THE FINACH

When I am very sad, I eat like a temperamental toddler. I don't want anything at all, and then I want one thing, and only that, in a certain bowl, and I want to eat it with a spoon. This spinach has all the things I crave at those times—mellow richness, but not too much, and mild spiciness with no heat, and a little umami tang from the bacon and miso. Plus, it is good for you, because: spinach. Which means no one can hassle you about eating again for a while. Zucchini Me-Mo (page 37) can also do a shift on the Vegetables for Sadness rotationas can half a cabbage, shredded and sautéed forever in ghee with a little salt and lemon zest. Butter, ghee, or coconut oil can stand-in for the bacon drippings, if for any number of valid reasons you don't hoard those.

SERVES 1 TO 4

2 tablespoons bacon drippings, unsalted butter, ghee, or coconut oil

2 medium shallots, minced (about ⅓ cup)

1 tablespoon smooth white miso paste

1 teaspoon mild curry powder

One 10-ounce package frozen chopped spinach, thawed

¼ cup heavy cream or coconut cream

Freshly ground pepper

1 Warm the bacon drippings in a medium skillet set over medium heat. Add the shallots and sauté for about 6 minutes, until it is soft and lightly browned.

2 Add the miso and curry, and stir to combine.

3 Add the spinach and cook, stirring, for a few minutes, then add the cream and a few grinds of pepper and stir well to coat the vegetables.

4 Keep at a low sizzle for another 2–3 minutes, until any excess liquid is cooked off and the sauce has thickened.

TAKE A DIP

Dip makes any plain thing that is baked (like bread or a potato) or roasted (such as a squash) into a rounder and tastier almost-meal. The muscle memory involved in dipping and eating, dipping and eating, can be enough to jump-start a faltering appetite. Along with punchy flavor, these two dips carry many elements of good nutrition, so if you're worried someone is not eating enough to keep a frigging bird alive, my goodness, then set a little plate of carrot twigs and a tiny bowl of dip near their elbow while they are doing something else. (The UnPeanut Sauce [page 27] and the Roasted Carrot Romesco [page 35] also work.) Both dips below call for a puree of preserved lemons, a briny, salty, tart miracle substance that is a pantry essential for me. Use green olives or capers in its place. All dips might accommodate a clove of garlic, but use your judgment; things that are strongly flavored or might have a long-lasting echo are things I avoid presenting to sad people unless I know they crave them.

GREEN GOODNESS

Tart and salty are mesmerizing flavors that balance nicely around the body provided by the seeds and greens. Soaking the seeds before blending is optional, but it improves digestibility and lends a creamier texture.

MAKES ABOUT 1½ CUPS

¾ cup sunflower seeds, soaked for 30 minutes or more in warm water to cover

1 big handful (about 1 ounce) baby spinach leaves

1 scant cup flat-leaf parsley leaves (tough stems discarded)

1 tablespoon Preserved Lemon Puree (page 68)

3 tablespoons lemon juice

1 teaspoon ground cumin

¼ teaspoon freshly ground pepper or cayenne pepper

⅓ cup good olive oil

1   Drain the seeds and add them to a blender or food processor along with the spinach, parsley, preserved lemons, lemon juice, cumin, and pepper. Blend, adding a few teaspoons of water if needed to get the mixture moving. With the machine running, add the oil in a steady stream and blend until smooth.

BIG DILL

Yogurt brings hearty tang and plenty of good nutrients like calcium, protein, and probiotics to this pretty green dip. For those avoiding dairy, soaked cashews make a good substitute for the yogurt.

MAKES ABOUT 1 CUP

1 romaine heart, darker green outer leaves reserved for another use (or the heart of a head of Bibb, Boston, or any other sturdy, mild lettuce)
1 bunch fresh dill

¼ cup any type plain Greek yogurt, or ¼ cup cashews, soaked in water for 1 hour and drained
1 teaspoon smoked or sweet paprika

1 tablespoon Preserved Lemon Puree (page 68)
½ cup good olive oil

1   Roughly chop the romaine heart and add it to a blender or food processor along with the dill, yogurt, paprika, and preserved lemons. Coarsely combine, and then with the machine running, add the oil in a steady stream and blend until smooth.

NAOMI AND LINA'S ALMOND COOKIES

Sometimes my friend Naomi shows up at my door with an empty peanut butter jar full of dahlias she has grown that are so glorious as to make a burlesque dancer blush, and when she sets them on the table and tosses a few hazelnuts from her tree, little trios of them still clustered in their curly green pods, around the base of the jar, I suddenly feel the value of my house increase in every possible way. And there was this one time she popped over with some cookies that her friend Lina used to make when she was a private chef for macrobiotic movie stars and popes and what have you. Even without their glam backstory, these are satisfying and nourishing, and the hint of spice makes them just interesting enough to provide a sliver of pleasure. The recipe doubles easily, which is good because the "dough" tastes so good that you may not be able to bake absolutely all of it.

MAKES ABOUT 18 COOKIES

1 cup raw almonds
¼ cup maple syrup
½ teaspoon kosher or
  flaky sea salt

½ teaspoon vanilla
  bean paste or vanilla
  extract
2 cardamom pods,
  shells removed, or

¼ teaspoon ground
  cardamom
2 teaspoons water

1   Preheat the oven to 325°F, and line a baking sheet with parchment paper.

2   Put the almonds, maple syrup, salt, vanilla, cardamom, and water in the bowl of a food processor and pulse until you have a coarsely ground, uniform mixture.

3 Using two teaspoons, compact small portions of the mixture into little egg-shaped balls. Place these onto the parchment-lined pan; they can be quite close together as they do not spread. Bake for about 20 minutes or until they are a nice golden color.

4 Once cool, store airtight at room temperature. These keep like a dream, and are also well suited to mailing. They can be frozen for up to 3 months.

OTHER WAYS TO DO IT

You can mix the nuts up in infinite ways. A mixture of cashews and almonds gives a tenderer and slightly richer result, and walnuts, pecans, and other candidates all play nicely with the flavors.

BARK WITH BITE

Chocolate, for many of us, is a go-to substance when it comes time to eat your feelings. When sadness means very little attention is being paid to eating well, and appetite is limited, it's good to get whole grains and protein in at every opportunity, and here we let chocolate play the role of facilitator. This bark is quite simple to make and pretty to look at, and something irresistible happens when buckwheat gets its crazy magic in the mixture. The ingredients may say "healthy snack" but the eating of it definitely emphasizes treat. These must be refrigerated (and are delicious frozen); they are melty if left for long at room temperature; see "Other Ways to Do It" for a more heat-tolerant variation.

MAKES ABOUT 20 PIECES

½ cup coconut oil

⅔ cup cocoa powder, sifted to remove any lumps

3 tablespoons agave syrup, honey, or maple syrup

1 teaspoon vanilla bean paste or vanilla extract

½ cup kasha (toasted whole buckwheat kernels)

½ cup broken pretzel bits (I use Glutino GF pretzels or sesame

rings to make this gluten-free)

½ cup broken pecans

⅓ cup chopped dried cherries

2 tablespoons minced crystallized ginger

2 teaspoons whole flax seeds

1 Line a small baking sheet or 8 × 8-inch pan with parchment paper.

2 Melt the coconut oil by placing it in a medium bowl set in a larger bowl or a pan containing hot (but not very hot) water.

3 Remove the bowl from its bath, and add the cocoa, agave, and vanilla to the oil; whisk to thoroughly combine.

4 Add the kasha, pretzels, pecans, cherries, ginger, and flax seeds, and use a rubber spatula to fold them in.

5 Scrape the chocolate mixture into the waiting pan. Smooth it out into a somewhat even layer.

6 Refrigerate for at least one hour.

7 Use a large sharp knife to cut the bark roughly into sections; including an assortment of piece sizes and all the scrappy bits makes it even more irresistible. Transfer them to an airtight container and keep refrigerated or frozen.

OTHER WAYS TO DO IT

- IN PLACE OF THE PECANS, CHERRIES, AND GINGER, SUBSTITUTE (IN EQUIVALENT AMOUNTS): SHELLED, ROASTED, UNSALTED PISTACHIOS; DRIED APRICOTS; AND CACAO NIBS. ALSO ADD 1 TABLESPOON FOOD-GRADE DRIED ROSE PETALS, CRUSHED.

- FOR A TREAT THAT IS LESS DEPENDENT ON REFRIGERATION, YOU CAN MAKE THESE WITH 8 OUNCES OF SEMISWEET OR BITTERSWEET CHOCOLATE IN PLACE OF THE OIL, COCOA, AND SWEETENER. CHOP THE CHOCOLATE AND, IN A BOWL SET OVER A PAN OF HOT WATER, MELT IT ALMOST COMPLETELY, THEN REMOVE FROM THE HEAT AND ALLOW THE RESIDUAL HEAT TO COMPLETE THE MELTING; THIS IS A VERSION OF TEMPERING, WHICH WILL PROTECT THE CHOCOLATE'S SHEEN AND CONSISTENCY WHEN IT SOLIDIFIES AGAIN.

A HOT DRINK OF SUBSTANCE

Atole is a beverage with ancient Aztec roots, often served as part of the Day of the Dead festivities and as a remedy for having taken a chill. With a kick of spice, a nourishing base of grain, and a soothing milkiness from dairy or coconut milk, atole is comfort food you can drink. With the addition of chocolate, atole becomes champurrado. Like its more well-known cousin horchata, and also like its savory brother from another mother, Congee (page 104), variations in the grain base are common enough in the places of origin to invite your own experimentation: try oat or rice flour if you seek an alternative to the corn. Without chocolate, this is a very soothing preparation; with chocolate, it is a treat with built-in sustenance. I suppose a splash of rum would not be wrong, if the circumstances seem to warrant it.

SERVES 4 TO 6

For the
BASE

½ cup masa harina
or corn flour
Generous pinch of
sea salt
3 cups water
1 cup cow's milk or
carton-type coconut
milk
3 tablespoons brown
sugar, maple syrup,
or honey

To
FLAVOR
(USE ANY OR ALL)

2–3 whole cardamom
pods, lightly crushed,
or 1 cinnamon stick
1 small dried red chili,
or ¼ teaspoon ground
ancho or cayenne
pepper
One 1-inch ribbon
orange zest, removed
with a vegetable
peeler

3.5 ounces dark
(65%) chocolate,
broken into pieces

To
GARNISH

Finely grated chocolate
Finely grated orange
zest
Maldon or other flaky
salt

1   Put the masa harina in a medium saucepan. Add the salt and then the water in a slow, thin stream, whisking constantly to avoid lumps. Bring to a simmer over medium heat.

2   Whisk in the milk, sugar, cardamom, chili, and zest.

3   Return to a simmer and reduce the heat to low. Continue to simmer gently, whisking constantly, for about 5 minutes, until the drink is thickened and infused with the flavorings. Discard the whole spices and zest, and whisk in the chocolate. Thin with additional milk or water, as needed, to create a too-thin-to-eat-with-a-spoon, thicker-than-your-average drink consistency. Taste, and adjust the sweetness and salt to your preference. Ladle into mugs, garnish as desired, and serve. You can refrigerate this for later reheating in a tightly lidded jar, but it definitely should be served warm. It will keep up to 3 days refrigerated; simply thin with a little more milk or water and whisk it over low to medium heat to serve.

NANA'S TINY PANCAKES

My mother was raised on the Hungarian and German Jewish food of her grandmothers, and after cooking her way into kitchen life with 1950s American food as a nineteen-year-old Navy wife, she mastered many of the arts of French and especially Italian cooking. In between her professional achievements as an educator, she cooked and cooked and cooked: basic everyday things (like pot roasts and chocolate pudding and blueberry pancakes) and elaborate, exotic, project-like things (like Chinese char siu bao, with her friend Millie). She taught me and my sisters not just how to cook but how to think about it, how to travel on our stomachs and, most importantly, how to use our hearts in the kitchen and make the kitchen the heart of our homes. If I had to pick only one thing, these ridiculously simple pancakes are what her love tastes like to me. The value of these in feeding a sad person is extensive: tiny foods are harder to resist, and these are best when made tiny, as in silver-dollar size; they are delicious and unassuming when unadorned, sort of like a tiny omelet, and extra delicious when festooned with a tempting dollop of jam. The tangy cottage cheese makes them both very moreish and very nourishing.

MAKES ABOUT 45 TINY PANCAKES; SERVES 2 TO 4

1 cup small-curd cottage cheese

3 eggs

¼ cup sweet rice flour

Scant ⅛ teaspoon salt

Scant ½ teaspoon finely grated lemon zest

Unsalted butter, to cook

Jam or honey, to serve

1 Combine the cottage cheese, eggs, flour, salt, and lemon zest in a medium bowl and whisk well.

2 Heat a griddle or frying pan over medium heat until a drop of water sizzles on contact.

3   Add a hazelnut-sized knob of butter to the pan and tilt to cover.

4   Drop the batter by scant tablespoons 2 inches apart on the griddle. Keeping the heat on the low side of medium, cook for about 2 minutes, until the underside is golden; flip carefully and cook the second side for about 1 minute. Serve warm or at room temperature with jam or honey.

5

FOOD FOR CHEER, DISTRACTION, AND CELEBRATION

A PARTY WITHOUT CAKE IS JUST A MEETING

JULIA CHILD

MOST OF THE TIME, I AM LOOKING FOR LESS BOTHER (AND FEWER POTS) IN THE KITCHEN. ON THE BIRTHDAYS FOR WHICH I AM RESPONSIBLE, HOWEVER, I AM ALL ABOUT THE HEART'S DESIRE AND THE TROUBLE IT TAKES TO MAKE IT APPEAR. THINGS I HAVE AGREED TO ATTEMPT INCLUDE, BUT ARE NOT LIMITED TO, A SIX-TIERED HEART-SHAPED LEMON CAKE WITH ROSES ON IT, A RACETRACK CAKE (CONVENIENTLY REQUESTED FOR AN EIGHTH BIRTHDAY), AND A CAKE SHAPED LIKE A BOSTON DUCK TOUR BOAT BUT PROMINENTLY FEATURING STRAWBERRIES. I CAN'T SAY THAT THESE DESSERTS WERE READY FOR A CENTERFOLD SPREAD, OR THAT I MAINTAINED GOOD CHEER THROUGHOUT THE STEPS REQUIRED FOR ASSEMBLY, BUT I'M ALWAYS WILLING TO TAKE A RUN AT WHATEVER IS REQUESTED. THAT'S WHAT BIRTHDAYS ARE FOR.

I n the studio of the mind, where the schematics for these things are drawn up, the frosting is always smooth, time is limitless, and my wrists are as supple as the decorating acrobatics require. Furthermore, in the mental run-through, someone else will be washing the pastry bags.

Reality always intrudes, and brings with her the news that I have never actually gotten around to taking that cake decorating class and that I only have about forty-seven minutes in real time to assemble the thing. She often brings insufficient frosting, too, as well as crumbly cake and lost utensils and other impediments to the successful manifestation of what my mind's eye has in its crosshairs. That's Reality's winsome ways for you.

Inevitably, no matter what I have told myself in advance, I break out in the Birthday Sweats. I forget that it doesn't matter whether the mother of one of my children's friends can make an edible, nay, utterly delicious scale reproduction of Buckingham Palace with teeny little Beefeaters marching around it, or whether my own reach has exceeded my grasp in ways that will be obvious to onlookers. What matters is how the birthday human receives it.

My son looked at his first birthday cake, a disk of plain cake with plain pureed apricots on top, like it was the most shockingly beautiful thing he had seen in all his twelve months of life. I have a favorite photo of him, jaw dropped, as a slice of it was presented. It is clear that he cannot believe his good fortune. That's generally the reaction I am going for: "How lucky and loved am I?"

I have three children, with a combined fifty-one birthdays between them as of this writing. I have made many, many cakes. My files are laced with pictures of birthday confections, some outta-the-park winners, some respectable, some passable, some lumpy and leaning. The grinning birthday human is inevitably the nicest thing in each picture, and not just because my children are gorgeous. It's also because their faces register the nugget: a fuss has been made, for them and to their tastes. This is where the joy is found, not (necessarily) in a dew-speckled and breathtakingly lifelike buttercream rose.

It's the fact of the fuss more than its scale or its outcome. Let that be your mantra. And if pastry is not your thing (or the recipient's), so be it. Anything your recipient couldn't get their mitts on without your intervention scores high on the treat register. A fabulous sauce or a basket of perfect fruits you've gone to some trouble to pick or source or deliver—these can be as memorable and delightful a windfall as an éclair or a portrait of their dog in ganache.

Taking aim at a new skill is another surefire path to treat success. If this is your day to try cheese making, or pasta rolling, or wild food foraging, or a whole new cuisine, or just some recipe you saw in the morning paper, then it's a good day to share the bounty with a friend in need of cheer or distraction. Even a wonky outcome will likely charm its beneficiary, because of that simple piece of magic: the gesture alone demonstrates that you were thinking of this person. As humans, we tend to lap that up. You know how nice it is when someone texts you to say they are thinking of you? When they show up with a snack, that feeling compounds.

But again, the item you present need not be exotic: a person trapped at their desk by a deadline and confining their intake to vending machine snacks and takeout is easy to impress with the most basic home-sourced calories (and maybe a cloth napkin or a bottle with a flower in it).

Say you know that the target of your attention, if she or he knew that no one was watching, would eat just the cheesy top off the mac and cheese, or the cookie dough but not the cookie, the crispy fried egg white but not the yolk. Whether you are celebrating someone's win or bringing light to a dark day, your work could not be simpler. Just indulge this person.

By way of example, not long ago my niece found herself very far under the weather during finals week. She was in the grips of the kind of ice cream craving that any of us who have been miserable, under deadline, or in college probably know well, but again—she was stuck in bed in her off-campus apartment. She was many blocks from commerce, several states away from me, and it was late at night. In the dim reaches of my mind, a small bell began ringing. Here is a place where technology can really be an ally. *Twenty minutes*, my friends. In *twenty minutes*, the Internet, a guy in a subcompact car, and whoever took the time to establish a GrubHub or DoorDash or BringMeThat in her college town conspired with me to present three pints of ice cream on her front steps, giving both giver and receiver extreme happiness and leaving me out of pocket about $25, plus gratuity—a pretty fair trade.

How you go about providing just the right thing at just the right moment will vary wildly from person to person, and season to season, and circumstance to circumstance. Sometimes our old pal Reality is also a harsh mistress of the gift-bringer: perhaps you won't have insider information to guide you to peel the top off the mac and cheese or source the fruit she's been hunting for ever since the end of her Peace Corps service in Honduras. Or you may face a limitation of another kind: maybe you will have nothing more than a hospital gift shop or corner deli to use as your source. Trust that the timing, and maybe a little humor (roses, Rolos, and *Rolling Stone* magazine; a necklace made of Lifesavers) will carry the day. Even if you can't swan in with something luscious or exotic, if the thing you bring shows you put a little thought into it, you have an excellent chance of adding light to the scene.

COOKIE DOUGH

There's much lamenting and rending of clothing in my house on the part of my oldest child when cookie dough gets baked. She has been heard to remark that baking cookies is "a waste of perfectly good food." To be clear, this same person is still willing to choke down a baked cookie, but it's licking the bowl that really speaks to her deepest appetites. This little mixture, infinitely adaptable to individual diets and preferences, is just the ticket for people like this, if you happen to know (or be) one. Note that you absolutely cannot bake this mixture into cookies. The pinch of baking soda is for that "I stole this from the baker" flavor and its presence is not meant to indicate that they are oven-ready. If you don't have oat flour around, just pulse a handful of rolled oats in a blender or grinder until relatively fine.

MAKES ABOUT A CUP

¼ cup brown sugar or coconut sugar

2 tablespoons unsalted butter, softened

⅛ teaspoon vanilla bean paste or vanilla extract

2 teaspoons cream (any type) or non-dairy creamer

5 tablespoons almond meal or oat flour

¼ teaspoon salt

Tiny pinch of baking soda

Optional
ADDITIONS

2–3 tablespoons chocolate chips

2 tablespoons raisins, dried cranberries, or dried cherries

2 tablespoons old-fashioned rolled oats

2 tablespoons brickle or toffee bits

1 In a medium mixing bowl, cream the sugar with the butter until very well combined.

2 Beat in the vanilla and cream, and then add the almond meal, salt, and baking soda, and mix well. Stir in any or all of the optional additions.

3 Refrigerate (up to 3 days) or freeze (up to 1 month) the dough in an airtight container.

OTHER WAYS TO DO IT

For vegan dough, replace the butter with 1 tablespoon coconut butter + 1 tablespoon coconut oil (cool enough to be in a solid state). And either use non-dairy creamer or 1 teaspoon flax meal, bloomed for a few minutes in 2 teaspoons water.

BUTTERCREAM FOR SADNESS AND CAKES

In the immediate aftermath of my sister's death, my niece marched into a bakery and convinced the counterperson to sell us a pound of chocolate buttercream, which we attacked with two spoons as soon as we got to the relative privacy of the car in the parking lot. That little sliver of time is so tender and dear that it lives inside a vault in my heart.

The secret to making buttercream without rage or despair is Marshmallow Fluff. Because I have a reputation as a person concerned with healthy eating to protect, I have invested a mildly absurd amount of energy in finding a workaround for this, and I can tell you these three things as a result:

1. THERE ARE COMMERCIAL COUSINS TO MARSHMALLOW FLUFF THAT OFFER A SLIGHTLY HEALTHIER PROFILE. AS OF THIS WRITING, ONE IS CALLED SUZANNE'S RICEMELLOW CREME AND THE OTHER IS CALLED TOONIE MOONIE. BOTH ARE UTTERLY INTERCHANGEABLE FOR FLUFF (EVEN IN YOUR PEANUT BUTTER SANDWICH), AND CAN BE MAIL-ORDERED IF YOUR LOCAL HEALTH FOOD SHOP DOES NOT STOCK THEM.

2. AFTER MUCH TRIAL AND ERROR, ALL VERY STICKY, I HAVE SETTLED ON A HOMEMADE ALTERNATIVE THAT SOUNDS IMPLAUSIBLE BUT IS SHOCKINGLY EASY TO MAKE. I CALL IT WHUFF (SEE BELOW).

3. GO AHEAD AND USE THE FLUFF. LIFE IS SHORT. PLEASURE IS RESTORATIVE. *USE THE FLUFF.*

MAKES 1 CUP

½ cup (1 stick) unsalted butter, room-temperature softened (not oily-soft)

1 cup Marshmallow Fluff or Whuff (recipe follows)

2 ounces (55g) bittersweet chocolate, melted and cooled to room temperature

Pinch of salt

1 Make sure all your ingredients are at about the same temperature.

2 In a medium-sized mixing bowl or the bowl of a stand mixer fitted with a whisk attachment, cream the butter well. Add the marshmallowness you've selected by the heaping tablespoonful as you continue to beat.

3 Once smoothly combined, scrape the chocolate into the bowl and beat again until uniform and fluffy.

4 Add the salt and cream and beat again.

5 Use immediately, or transfer to an airtight container to refrigerate (1–3 days) or freeze (1–3 months) for later use. Bring to absolute room temperature (no chill) and beat again if you plan to use it to frost a cake. If you plan to use it to eat your feelings, no re-beating is necessary, and you get to decide the optimal temperature for consumption.

OTHER WAYS TO DO IT

In place of the chocolate, you can also flavor the buttercream with ⅓ cup Lemon Curd (page 153) or the same amount of a tart raspberry puree.

WHUFF

Marshmallow spread! There it is, on the shelf of every grocery and convenience store. You absolutely do not need to make your own. However, doing so certainly provides a morale boost, especially using the hocus-pocus here.

MAKES ABOUT 2 CUPS

One 15-ounce can chickpeas or white beans, with or without salt

½ cup sugar
½ teaspoon agar powder
Scant ⅛ teaspoon cream of tartar

¼ teaspoon vanilla bean paste or vanilla extract

1 Open the can of chickpeas and drain the liquid into a measuring cup, reserving the chickpeas for another use. You want ⅓ cup of this liquid and you can discard the rest. Place the liquid, the sugar, and the agar powder in a small pot and whisk to combine. Heat, stirring, over low to medium heat until the sugar is dissolved and the mixture comes to a low boil, about 3 minutes.

2 Pour the mixture into stand mixer fitted with a whisk attachment, or a large mixing bowl, and allow to cool completely. Add the cream of tartar and vanilla, and beat on high speed for 9–12 minutes, until you have a thick, white fluffy substance that stands right up in the bowl.

3 Stored airtight at in the fridge, Whuff will keep for about 3 days.

LEMON CURD

My friend Laura lives in San Diego, where passion fruits tumble disruptively onto her ping-pong table and lemons and limes are so bountiful as to be almost a nuisance. So, despite my East Coast address, I know that there is absolutely nothing like a lemon that reaches you seventy-two hours after being picked, sun-ripe, from someone who loves you at least enough to mail you boxes of lemons.

Lemon curd is one of the best things to do with lemons when you have a bunch of them, and it freezes so well that you can make one episode of preparing it last and last. Use it to make Mousse (page 155) or Buttercream (page 150); spoon it into a tart or meringue shell and top with blueberries—or any other berry, for that matter; or serve it with scones. Rose Levy Beranbaum, author of *The Cake Bible*, was the one who freed me from the idea that lemon curd was tricky or required any special equipment. Once I moved from all-yolks to whole eggs, eliminating a slightly metallic taste that bothers many people in a classic curd, even the lemon curd–resistant people in my orbit began to snuffle it up.

MAKES ABOUT 2 CUPS

4 eggs
1⅓ cups sugar
1 cup fresh lemon juice
(from 6–8 lemons)

Finely grated zest
of 3 lemons (about
3 tablespoons)

¾ cup (1½ sticks)
unsalted butter, cut
into 1-inch bits

1 Place a fine-mesh strainer over a medium bowl near your stove. A fine-mesh strainer is key: the silkiness of the end result depends on it, and this is all about silkiness.

2 Whisk together the eggs and sugar in a heavy saucepan. The sugar will protect the eggs from curdling when you add the lemon juice.

recipe continues

3 Now whisk in the lemon juice and zest, and then add the butter. Cook over low to medium heat, stirring all the time with a wooden spoon, for about 4 minutes, until the mixtures thickens and pales and nicely coats the back of the spoon. Keep it from boiling—if it begins to threaten boiling, raise the pot off the burner while you turn down the flame—but otherwise do not fret much about how things are going, as long as you keep stirring.

4 When it reaches spoon-coating thickness (it will continue to thicken as it cools, so that's as far as you need to take it), immediately dump it into the waiting strainer and force it through. All manner of eggy nubbins and lemon parts will stay behind in the strainer, and you should have a lovely, satiny curd in the bowl—unless you did not believe me about the fine-mesh strainer and tried to get by with something else.

5 If you want little flecks of yellow zestiness to perk things up visually, you can stir in another few scrapings of zest at this point.

6 It will keep 1 week or more in the fridge, and well longer than that in the freezer; simply thaw completely and then whisk to restore its silky texture.

OTHER WAYS TO DO IT

Make raspberry-lime curd by substituting 1 cup of frozen raspberries and ½ cup of lime juice for the lemon juice, and use lime zest instead of lemon zest.

A HERD OF MOUSSE

Here's the thing about mousse: it whips up in a jiffy, and you can do something no fancier than scoop it into a jar and maybe put some plain whipped cream on top of it and you will win friends and influence people. You can also use any flavor of it as a filling for a cake. Instructions follow for that assembly; you'll only need a dollop or two of the mousse to make that happen, and with the rest you can carry on as instructed here. No matter the flavor you are making, it's wise to hold aside a tablespoon or so of cream unwhipped; if you space out and overbeat your cream, as long as you haven't started to make butter, just softly stirring in some plain cream will pull it back from the edge.

COFFEE MOUSSE

Coffee and cream go together so well that they appear frequently as a duo in song titles and valentines. If caffeinated treats are a no-go, turn to one of the many substitutes available. Because my daughter loved the flavor of coffee from tiny tot–hood, we sampled many, and Dandy Blend proved hands down the winner. I once served this coffee-flavored mousse under a whipped-cream hat in little chocolate cups, like a dream about cappuccino, in lieu of birthday cupcakes, and that worked out pretty well.

MAKES ABOUT 5 CUPS

- ½ cup sugar
- 1 tablespoon instant coffee or coffee substitute (see headnote)
- ¼ cup cornstarch
- 1½ cups whole milk
- 2 cups heavy cream
- Crumbled chocolate cookies or chocolate shavings, to serve (optional)

recipe continues

1   Add the sugar, coffee, and cornstarch to a small saucepan and mix until free of lumps and well combined.

2   Slowly add the milk, stirring all the while, and mix until smooth. Cook over medium heat, stirring constantly, and continue cooking until it thickens obviously, about 3 minutes total.

3   Pour into a medium bowl (one that is a bit too large for this quantity), and press a piece of waxed or parchment paper right onto the surface to prevent a skin from forming as it cools. Cool it down at least to room temperature, or refrigerate if you have time (and for up to 3 days, if you'd like to prepare it ahead).

4   Whip the cream using vigilance and attention to soft peaks. *Soft.* Reserve about a quarter of the whipped cream in a separate bowl (or drop it into a pastry bag if you are feeling fancy).

5   Using a balloon whisk, fold a dollop of the whipped cream into the cooled coffee mixture, to lighten it, then lightly but thoroughly combine the two mixtures. Scrape into one large or several individual dishes, and garnish with the reserved plain whipped cream. Refrigerate for as long as you can stand to wait; a couple of hours is ideal (and it will keep up to 2 days in the refrigerator).

6   Top with crumbled chocolate cookies or chocolate shavings, for a special touch.

LEMON MOUSSE

A mousse made by just combining lemon curd and whipped cream is such a great thing that you don't have to extend yourself any further than that. But adding a really fresh, creamy ricotta will bring an almost-cheesecake mood to the party, along with, you know, lots of calcium and protein, which is of course the main reason anyone wants to eat mousse.

MAKES ABOUT 4 CUPS

1 cup Lemon Curd
  (page 153)
¾ cup ricotta
1 cup heavy cream

¼ cup powdered sugar,
  sifted
1 lime
1 pint raspberries

2–3 tablespoons
  granulated sugar

1   Combine the lemon curd and ricotta in a large bowl.

2   In a separate bowl, whip the cream and powdered sugar to soft peaks.

3   Reserve about a quarter of the whipped cream for garnish. Using a balloon whisk, fold a dollop of the whipped cream into the ricotta-lemon curd mixture, to lighten it, then lightly but thoroughly combine the two mixtures. Scrape the mousse into one large or several individual dishes, and garnish with the reserved plain whipped cream. Refrigerate for 2 hours or up to 2 days.

4   Using a Microplane, zest a lime onto the surface of the dish or dishes.

5   While the mousse chills, juice the lime, and in a small bowl toss the raspberries with the lime juice and sugar. Spoon a little of the berries and their accumulated juices over each serving.

CHOCOLATE ROSE MOUSSE

Odds are good I don't need to campaign for chocolate mousse. But I will say that a version without the traditional egg yolks is a little lighter on the system, and the addition of a hint (really no more than a hint) of roses and olive oil makes an already light-ish substance positively ethereal.

MAKES ABOUT 4 CUPS

6 ounces semi- or bittersweet chocolate

1 tablespoon excellent olive oil

2 cups heavy cream, divided

½ teaspoon vanilla bean paste or vanilla extract

½ teaspoon rosewater (optional)

½ pint raspberries, to serve (optional)

1 Chop the chocolate and put it into a medium-sized mixing bowl with the olive oil. Have ready a larger bowl of ice water, or a cold pack large enough to rest the mixing bowl on, and six or seven small cups (or more—shot glasses would work, too) to receive the finished product, as well as a folded towel.

2 In a small saucepan, heat 1 cup of the cream to a simmer (crowds of small bubbles at the edge of the pan). Dump the hot cream over the chocolate mixture. Let this stand a minute, undisturbed, so the chocolate will melt. Whisk until smooth.

3 Place the bowl with the chocolate mixture over the ice water or cold pack, and continue whisking until the mixture cools and begins to thicken. This will take approximately forever, or about 6 minutes. It will not seem to be doing anything at all for the first 5.2 minutes, and then, when it is indeed finally chilled, your silky liquid will rapidly begin to thicken. You want to stop as soon as whisk marks are visible when you pause.

4   Immediately spoon the thickened chocolate into the waiting cups, and rap them gently on the folded towel to settle and even the mousse.

5   If you are using a portion of this to fill Teeny Cake (page 162), this is the stage at which you want to siphon off that amount, and spread it before it sets. Regardless, *do not* scrape the chocolate bowl out clean. Be careful to leave about ¼ to ⅓ cup of chocolate in the bowl.

6   Add the remaining cream to this messy situation, along with the vanilla and the rosewater, if using. Beat this combination until you have softly whipped cream. Divide the whipped cream among the little pots of mousse and again, rap them gently to level them off.

7   Raspberries make a lovely fillip on the top, but you won't miss them if they aren't there. If you find you have to chill the mousse until later (it will keep for up to 2 days), cover the container(s) tightly to prevent the top of the cream from drying or absorbing fridge odors, and let stand for about 30 minutes at room temperature before eating. Promise me you will try, at least, because the subtleties of the olive oil and rose are most evident when the chill is off.

SHAPESHIFTER BAKED PANCAKE

This is comfort food of the highest order. Served warm from the oven with some fruit and cream, fragrant with vanilla and a hint of lemon and just an overall home-baked quality, it's certain to make sad people feel cared for and happy people feel celebrated. It's dessert and it's breakfast and it's I want something yummy right now. Once it cools, you can also use it to make Teeny Cake (page 162)—further compounding its value by cutting, filling, and frosting it.

MAKES ONE 10-INCH PANCAKE

2 tablespoons unsalted
  butter
4 eggs, separated
Pinch of salt

¼ cup sugar
Barest scrape finely
  grated lemon zest
5 tablespoons sweet
  rice flour

Jam or cream, to serve
(optional)

1   Preheat the oven to 350°F.

2   Put the butter into a 10-inch ovenproof skillet, and begin to heat it on the stove over low heat.

3   In a clean, dry bowl, use a balloon whisk or mixer to beat the egg whites with the salt until glossy and peaked.

4   In a separate bowl, beat the egg yolks with the sugar and lemon zest until thick and pale, about 4 minutes by hand with a balloon whisk.

5   Turn the heat up a little under the pan, to prepare it to receive the batter.

6   Now fold a little of the egg whites into the yolk mixture to lighten, then begin to fold in the remainder, and when it's about half combined, sprinkle the flour over the mixture. Gently fold until well blended, and pour into the waiting pan, where the butter should be foamy. Slide into the hot oven.

7   Bake for 16–20 minutes, until lightly golden on top and springy to the touch in the center.

8   Serve right away, from the pan, with a dollop of jam and cream, or take it neat.

9   To use it for tiny cakes, loosen the edges with a thin spatula and spread a sheet of wax or parchment paper on a baking rack. Hold the rack firmly to the top of the pan and invert the pancake onto the paper to cool completely.

TEENY CAKE

My friend Peggy is a master baker, and I do not toss this term out lightly. She is a professional pastry chef and published expert on the subject. Early in our friendship, when I heard that her birthday was on the horizon, I asked who made (as in, who dared to make) her birthday cake. She paused. No one, she said. Not since tiny girlhood, when she presumably began making croquembouche in her Easy-Bake Oven, had someone even tried. My love of treating overcame my feelings of inadequacy. Teeny Cake can do that for you, and more.

Making a teeny cake is far less daunting for the maker than a grand creation that is destined to serve a crowd, and even if the thing turns out ever so slightly wonky, it is likely to charm. This holds true for scaled-down versions of just about anything. All manner of resistance has been known to melt in the face of a magically miniature offering on a plate. Why is a teeny cake better than a cupcake, you might ask? Well, because cupcakes are everywhere these days, for one thing, and for another: because it is a teeny mouse-sized cake and that is better than a cupcake.

NOTE: *If the cake will wait a while before being consumed (in which case, it could absorb too much moisture from the mousse), or if you like the flavor possibilities, be sure to include the optional jam when you assemble the cake.*

MAKES 1 TEENY CAKE

1 Shapeshifter Baked
   Pancake (page 160)
1 batch Mousse, any
   flavor (page 155)

1 batch Buttercream
   (page 150)
Small amount jam
   (apricot or raspberry
   are favorites; optional)

Fresh berries, fresh
   flowers, small chocolates,
   candy, crushed cookies,
   toffee, or nuts, to
   decorate

1 Using a round cookie or biscuit cutter, about 3 inches in diameter, or a thin-walled drinking or wine glass of about that size, cut two or three circles from the cake.

2 Create a cake plate by wrapping a 5-inch cardboard circle (cut from a sturdy paper plate or cardboard) with aluminum foil. Drop a teaspoon of the buttercream in the center of the plate, to secure the cake, and place the first cake layer on top of it. Spread a very thin layer of jam on this layer, then drop about 1 tablespoon of mousse in the center and spread it out evenly, stopping just before the edges. Take the next layer in hand, and spread a thin layer of jam on one side; plop it jam side down on top of the mousse, taking care not to press. If you'd like to make a three-layer cake, jam the top of the cake layer you just placed and repeat the steps, ending with a layer of cake that has jam underneath and is bare on top. It's a good idea, if time permits, to refrigerate the stack for about 30 minutes to solidify, but it's not absolutely necessary.

3 Working with absolutely room-temperature buttercream, and using about a tablespoon at a time and a very light hand, begin to cover the sides, then the top of the stack with an even coating. For the neatest result, make this layer a thin one (it's okay if cake shows through in spots), and let the cake rest in the fridge again, for about 10 minutes, to firm. This is called a crumb coat, and it functions as a kind of primer so you can spread the final layer more smoothly. It's completely optional. Frost the cake with the final covering, making it smooth or swoopy or running the tines of a fork across it as suits your mood of the moment.

4 When you're done with that, it's time to festoon the cake with any of your chosen decorative elements. Make sure to chill the wee item thoroughly before transporting it any farther than from one room to the next, and also to bring it to room temperature before serving.

HOW CORDIAL

A pretty bottle of fruit syrup is a welcome sight on a sweltering day, especially when paired with a bottle of sparkling water; it's basically a little desert oasis you can present to a hot person. But the appeal of this pairing is not lost on other kinds of people: nursing mothers, parched and recovering people, people in want of a cocktail, and people wishing to celebrate, but with a mocktail that feels more like a step up from alcohol than a consolation prize. All of these people (and more) are likely to greet the lovely hue and tantalizing scent of these cordials with enthusiasm. Tucking a nourishing herb in among the big flavors makes it easy to reap its rewards.

MAKES ABOUT 1 QUART

4 cups water

1 cup sugar, honey, or agave syrup

1 pound peaches, sliced, intact pits included

1 sprig fresh basil

1 tablespoon finely grated fresh turmeric root

Juice of 1–2 lemons (about ¼–⅓ cup)

1   Combine the water and sugar in a large saucepan and bring to a boil, stirring until the sweetener is dissolved. Add the peaches and lower the heat to a simmer, cooking undisturbed until the fruit gives it all up but has not disintegrated—somewhere around 5 minutes, depending on its ripeness.

2   Remove from the heat, drop the basil and turmeric into the pot, cover, and let steep for 5 minutes.

3 Strain the mixture through a fine-mesh sieve and add the lemon juice. Taste for sweetness and adjust as needed, remembering that this will be substantially diluted at serving time. Store in a bottle or jar in the refrigerator and serve over ice with a generous amount of sparkling or still water. This will keep for about 5 days.

OTHER WAYS TO DO IT

Here are some other fruit and herb combinations to try:

- STRAWBERRY + CHILI + MINT

- RHUBARB + GINGER + LEMONGRASS

- PEAR + CORIANDER SEED + NETTLE

BUCKWHEAT SLAB CRACKERS

As the Savory Granola (page 192) can attest, treats don't always have to be sweet. A basket or cellophane bag of these beauties, with a round or wedge of cheese, a few olives, maybe a bunch of grapes or some dried figs, is a gorgeously welcome interruption to someone's day. Hazelnuts and pumpkin seeds are excellent stand-ins for the pecans if you want to mix it up. A note that the grain-cooking step that starts things off here produces twice as much as you need for the crackers because I have yet to figure out how to successfully cook a smaller amount than that; unless you have a teeny tiny pot in your kitchen or are starting with grain cooked for another reason (this is a great way to deploy leftover cooked rice), you can either freeze half the cooked grain for the next batch of crackers you make, or enjoy a hot snack to fuel your cracker-rolling.

MAKES 16 CRACKERS

¼ cup millet

¼ cup white rice

1½ cups boiling water

¼ cup (42g) flax seeds

½ cup water

1⅓ cups (130g) coarsely chopped pecans

1¼ cup (150g) buckwheat flour

1 teaspoon baking powder

1½ teaspoons sea salt

A hefty twist of freshly ground pepper

1 tablespoon maple syrup

¼ cup olive oil, plus more to finish

1 tablespoon rice vinegar

2–4 tablespoons water

Maldon or other flakey salt, to finish

1   In a small saucepan, dry-toast the millet and rice by stirring and shaking over medium heat until the grains emit a toasty fragrance and are barely golden in color, about 3 minutes. Add the boiling water, bring to a simmer, and then cook, covered, over lowest heat until the

water is absorbed, about 15 minutes. Let stand, covered, to fully steam the grains, another 5 minutes. Fluff with a fork and set aside to cool.

2   Put the flax seeds to soak in a small bowl with ½ cup of cold water.

3   Toast the nuts in a dry skillet or warm oven, until fragrant and lightly golden; remove to a dish to cool.

4   Preheat the oven to 425°F. Have ready two baking sheets and four sheets of parchment paper, cut to fit.

5   Combine ¾ cup of the cooked grains, buckwheat flour, 1 cup of the pecans (reserve the remainder for later), soaked flax seeds, baking powder, salt, and pepper in the bowl of a food processor and pulse one or two times to blend. add the maple syrup, oil, and vinegar and give another 10 pulses to evenly combine the ingredients; the mixture should look pebbly. Scrape down the sides, add 2 tablespoons of water, and then let the mixer run for a full minute. This should create a thick, unsticky dough that clumps together in a ball; you can add an additional teaspoon of water, a dribble at a time, to make this happen if the dough seems too dry to come together, but give it a full minute before you resort to that.

6   Remove the dough ball to a piece of wax paper and sprinkle the reserved pecans on top. Briefly knead the dough to incorporate these, then form a smooth disk. Wrap this snugly in wax paper and refrigerate for at least 30 minutes, or up to a full day. (You can also freeze the dough for up to a month.)

7   Cut the disk, pie-style, into 16 wedges.

recipe continues

8   With a long side of the parchment rectangle at the top of your work area, set four wedges of dough evenly spaced across it. Cover with another parchment sheet and use the palm of your hand to partially flatten each wedge, then use a rolling pin to roll away from you, then toward you, transforming the wedges into four knobby oblongs that are roughly ¼-inch thick. It's okay if they are quite close together; they do not spread while baking. This is a time to embrace odd shapes and throw all thought of straight edges to the four winds; the irregular shape and slightly varied thickness are the magic here. Peel off the top parchment, reserving it to use again, and slide the crackers onto the baking sheet. Repeat for the other baking sheet.

9   Brush the surfaces lightly with olive oil and sprinkle with the coarse salt, pressing to adhere it.

10   Bake 5–6 minutes, rotating the sheets back to front and upper to lower to ensure even baking. Carefully flip the crackers over, returning them to the oven for an additional 2–3 minutes to finish browning.

11   Repeat with the remaining dough, using the baking time of the first sheets to roll out the next batch. It's fine to plop the parchment sheet of dough directly onto an already-hot baking pan, as long as you slip it into the oven right away. Cool the crackers completely before storing in an airtight container.

ICE CREAM SHELL GAME

You can make a tasty "magic" ice cream shell by melting together two parts coconut oil to three parts chocolate. Or you can make this. Maple and cocoa bring a fudgier texture to a shell that still has some snap; the chili brings heat, and the bacon brings bacon. For the bacon-averse, use a smoky chili, like a dried chipotle.

MAKES ABOUT 1 CUP

½ cup coconut oil, including (or not) 2 tablespoons bacon fat
3–4 dried red bird chili peppers, broken open,

or 2 teaspoons crushed red pepper flakes
1 tablespoon black or Dutch-process cocoa powder
Tiny pinch of sea salt

1 tablespoon maple syrup
5 ounces dark (66–72%) chocolate, chopped
Ice cream, to serve

1   Combine the oil and chili peppers in a heatproof bowl, and set over simmering water to infuse for 5 minutes. Remove from the heat and let stand at room temperature for another 5 minutes; the oil should have a nice orange hue. Strain out and discard the solids and return the infused oil to the bowl.

2   Add the cocoa, salt, and maple syrup to the oil and whisk until smooth, then add the chocolate. Return the bowl to its perch over the simmering water and heat, stirring, until smooth.

3   Transfer the chocolate dip to a squeeze bottle or container and store at room temperature. It stiffens if it has to stand at room temperature very long, but a brief stint in hot water will make it pourable again.

4   Pour over ice cream and let stand for about 30 seconds before eating. The mixture can be kept for a month at room temperature.

To:
From:

6

FOOD
FOR LUNCH BOXES
AND
CARE PACKAGES

IT IS MORE FUN
TO TALK WITH
someone who doesn't use
long, difficult words but
rather short, easy words,
LIKE "WHAT ABOUT
LUNCH?"
A. A. MILNE

I WAS WAITING IN THE PICK-UP LANE FOR MY CHILDREN ON A FINE DAY IN THE EARLY FALL, SCANNING THE CROWD OF BEAUTIFUL CHILDREN FOR MY QUARRY. MY EYE LANDED ON A BOY ABOUT MY SON'S AGE WHOSE PERSONAL THING, AS A FRIEND OF MINE USED TO SAY, WAS TOTALLY NOT TOGETHER. HIS JACKET WAS HALF-ON AND ABOUT THREE-QUARTERS OFF, SHIRT UNTUCKED, HAIR ASKEW. HIS LUNCH BOX—LIKELY CAREFULLY SELECTED FROM ONE OF THE FANCY-PANTS LUNCH-PACKING BOUTIQUES, POSSIBLY EMBROIDERED WITH HIS NAME, AND UNDOUBTEDLY LOVINGLY PACKED WITH ORGANIC TREATS—FOLLOWED BEHIND HIM BY A GOOD TWO FEET, ITS CONVENIENT AND STURDY WEBBING STRAP YANKED TO ITS FULLEST LENGTH AND HELD CASUALLY IN ONE OF HIS HANDS. I WATCHED IT BUMP ALONG THE GROUND, HOP OVER LANDSCAPING STONES WHEN IT TRAILED INTO A FLOWER BED, AND LEGIT GET DRAGGED *THROUGH A PUDDLE* BEFORE CONTINUING ON TO THE SCHOOL BUS UP THE—*BUMP, BUMP, BUMP*—STEPS. I IMAGINED HIS MOTHER RECEIVING ALL OF THIS ON HER END, COMPARING THE TIDY, COMBED, AND TUCKED FELLOW SHE DROPPED OFF IN THE MORNING TO THE CHOCOLATE MESS SHE WAS COLLECTING FROM THE BUS STOP. I HAD A CLEAR PICTURE IN MY MIND'S EYE OF HER FACIAL EXPRESSION AS SHE EXAMINED THE ONCE-PRISTINE BPA-FREE LUNCH BOX. SURELY THE SCHOOL WOULD HAVE CALLED IF THE SECOND GRADE HAD BEEN AMBUSHED BY BEARS?

T he thought bubble I imagined over her head read: *Why bother?* Why bother making food look or taste especially nice? Why take any trouble at all? For a utilitarian purpose like a boxed lunch, in particular, it's easy to wonder (especially late in the week, or any day of any week that takes place after spring vacation, or when the lunch box turns up looking like an "after" picture) if there's any point to making the effort. The beneficiary of the packed meal is likely to scarf it down in five minutes anyway, because it's just fuel for the next phase of whatever pursuit has rendered them dependent on portable food for sustenance.

Here's what I think. Food is fuel, to be sure; we can't live without a certain number and type of calories daily. But we aren't combustion engines, and we aren't amoebas. While food doesn't have to be, and probably shouldn't be, anyone's reason for living, humans are organisms whose senses and emotions and health are all intricately connected. When food, and our experience of eating it, makes us think for a minute about being loved, or about where it came from, or about how fine it is to taste something that makes us pause to appreciate it in our mouths, then we are not just refueling. We are reconnecting. We are adding a little more light and life to our condition, whatever it may be, and maybe even knitting back up the raveled sleeve of whatever cares have worn us down, should there happen to be any.

"Here is something to eat," says the packed-up nutrition, "and with it the knowledge that someone was thinking of you, is looking out for you, has translated their caring thoughts into substantive care of the most accessible type for any animal." This applies even if the advance packer and the ultimate consumer are the same person. Your morning self can pack your later-on self a nice, satisfying lunch and then you get fed *and* get in your own good graces, a cosmic double win.

At least for people looking after students and office workers and others who require meals away from home roughly every Monday through Friday, the demands of the lunch box are relentless. It's *every day* with the lunch box. Furthermore, in its quest to batter you down, it does not work alone. Its partners in crime include dueling soccer games and violin lessons, mealtime dance classes and after-hours meetings. Anyone who stares down the preparation of three meals a day for as many people as live under their roof faces a few moments in that week when What Is Needed is not exactly What's On Hand. Advance preparation is a big boost to meeting this challenge.

I like to shore up my defenses on Sunday. I don't always make good on this intention, but when I do, the week seems to unfurl with a little less twitching and gasping at Pack the Calories time. A monstrous pot of beans or soup, a batch of fruit tapioca, baked custard, or chocolate pudding—these are all Sunday money in the midweek bank. And if I can siphon off a little bit of the soup or beans into a freezer container, even better.

In my fonder moments, I think of the lunch box as a care package I pack every day. More commonly, I say rude things about it or wake up with mental whitespace where there ought to be a list of what I can possibly manifest to put inside it. There were moments during the years that I had three school-age children, especially toward the spring term, when the lunch box haunted my dreams. But it is certainly the place where the tools of the to-go trade get a solid workout. And because I know that lunch boxes wear me down, when a chill settles around my lunch-packing heart, when I head to bed in a house full of containers whose lids have been lost or are unwashed and yet must be filled again when the sun rises, I resort to low-tech forms of hocus-pocus. I know we are not supposed to trick young eaters and it's wrong to play games with food. I also know how a grumpy person (of any age) perks up when you scratch a note into the banana or put facial features on their sandwich. (Olives! Can't be beat for this sort of shenanigans.) Eating is supposed to be a happy thing, after all.

Maybe some of you are saying, but lunch is a sandwich, a drink, and a piece of fruit (or whatever the default setting is on your lunch plan). If a meal needs to please the senses, gawd help me, let it be dinner, and let's let lunch just be lunch, because I need lunch to be fast. There's merit to this line of reasoning. I am not advocating that we all join the ranks of the crazed Bento moms who have aspic cutters and the blogs to prove they are not afraid to use them, creating vivid reenactments of treasured animated films out of rice and cold cuts. But with the addition of little more than three minutes to the total preparation time, most lunch-box tricks pack a huge cost/benefit ratio. Are you packing fruit salad? Poke it onto a skewer. And part of their magic lies in the fact that any magic these tricks possess depends on infrequency; if you used cookie cutters on the sandwich every day, it would dull the sparkle of finding a bunny where a triangle is expected. Nobody wants to read a love note on the banana (scratch it into the peel lightly with a pencil or even a fat needle; your message darkens magically by the time the lunch is opened) or the orange (use the channel knife that came in that bartending kit you got nine Christmases ago) *every day*. That edges toward the creepy. But there is something about lifting the fog of drudgery on the packing of the meal with some little act of silliness that also lifts the spirits of both preparer and consumer.

I definitely have a happier relationship with the more traditional interpretation of the care package, the version that calls up memories of mail-call at summer camp and involves affixing postage and honing your sense of how transit time and shipping method will affect the contents. It is a pretty comparable exercise, though. Because, lunch box or flat-rate Priority Mail carton, the message is the same: "Thinking of you!/You should eat a little!" And like fancy touches in the lunch box, the care package gets a lot of its power from its *rara avis* status. Most days, whether those days are spent at an office or at what my one daughter used to call "sleep-away college," mail is *meh*. Junk mail, bills, and announcements of one sort or another make up the lion's share, their contents pretty obvious and in some way burdensome. But a box! A box is an event. You have to balance it on your bike or your lap or clutch it in some obvious fashion as you make your way back to your cabin, desk, or dorm room. At least mentally, you are rubbing your hands together in greedy glee.

As I move through regular life, I collect all kinds of doodads to keep in my stash of care-package material. I like a box to feature a balance of homemade (some durable cookie- or brownie-esque item), humorous (hello, novelty erasers and temporary belly-button tattoos), and exotic (sachets of fancy French cocoa, for example, or most of what's available in the candy aisle of a large Asian grocery store). I like to throw in some health-giving item, such as an herbal tea or essential oil or clean socks. Cushion the contents with a foreign-language newspaper or the funnies. There's probably room for a silly photo or bad limerick. *Boom*. You are now the hero of the mailbag.

FORSAKING ALL OTHERS ROASTED TOMATO SOUP

I've had the same copies of the Moosewood Cookbook and The Enchanted Broccoli Forest since dinosaurs roamed the earth; the pages have the splatters and dog-ears to prove it. From the all-day-project magnitude of eggplant moussaka to the poetic simplicity of baked custard, there is reliability on every page. Your house will smell good and the food will taste good and everything will be fine—that is Moosewood cooking, to me. Even after years of traveling together, I can still find surprises in those books, such as the genius move I discovered long after I thought anyone needed to tell me how to make tomato soup, of adding a little bit of honey and mayonnaise to it. The flavors balance magically and ho-hum tomato soup becomes the tangy tomato soup of your best grilled-cheese memory. "Oh, thanks a lot," said my younger daughter when I made this vegetable-enhanced version. "Now I can't ever eat any other tomato soup ever again." It's a lunch box staple and holds up to giant-batch/stash-it-in-the-freezer preparations. If you are serving it in a bowl and not a thermos, you can gild the lily by providing a drizzle of lemon oil or minced fennel fronds or some crème fraîche or casually rustic crumbles of goat cheese, but you won't miss those touches if you skip them. The soup is remarkably tastier on its second day, so don't be afraid to make it ahead.

MAKES ABOUT 12 CUPS

1 medium fennel bulb, trimmed of stalks and cut into 1- to 2-inch chunks

2 large carrots, peeled and cut into 1- to 2-inch chunks

2 tablespoons olive oil

Coarse salt and freshly ground pepper

2 tablespoons unsalted butter or olive oil

2 cloves garlic, finely chopped

One 28-ounce can ground peeled tomatoes

6 cups water

One 6-ounce jar artichoke hearts, drained

recipe continues

1 tablespoon honey	**To**	Crème fraîche
3 tablespoons Vegenaise or mayonnaise	**GARNISH** (OPTIONAL)	Goat cheese crumbles
1½ teaspoons salt	A drizzle of lemon oil	
	Minced fennel fronds	

1 Preheat the oven to 400°F. Line a rimmed baking sheet with parchment paper. Toss the fennel and carrots with the olive oil, spread them on the tray in a single layer, and sprinkle a bit of salt and pepper over them. Roast for about 15 minutes, until they are starting to brown at the edges, then toss them with a spatula and switch the oven off; leave the vegetables in the oven to soften a little more in the residual heat as you get on with the other preparations.

2 Heat the butter in a large pot over low–medium heat, and sauté the garlic in it for about 1 minute, being careful not to let it brown. Add the tomatoes and heat them through. Add the roasted vegetables along with the water and the artichoke hearts. Simmer for 15–20 minutes, until the carrots and fennel are tender enough to cut with a spoon.

3 Now attack the soup with an immersion blender, or process in batches in a regular blender, observing all commonsense precautions regarding hot liquid and expansion, until you have a thick, smooth puree.

4 Whisk in the honey along with the Vegenaise, and taste to correct the seasoning as you like.

5 This soup can be used immediately, refrigerated for up to a week, or frozen for up to 3 months.

POCKET FRITTATAS

"Don't think I am fooled by the whole muffin thing," said my eldest, the Chief Resident Quinoa Skeptic, in dark tones, when I served these. "I can see they are made of quinoa." But before I could respond in any way, she had eaten it. And then she ate another. They come across like something between a nice, not-at-all dry muffin and an amusingly portable frittata. They are tasty hot, with a big messy salad and maybe some soup, for dinner, but they also ride happily at room temperature into lunch boxes or other places food gets grabbed and consumed on the fly. Like a frittata, quiche, or omelet, they are kind of a blank canvas, and a list of variations follows the main recipe.

MAKES 12

1 tablespoon neutral vegetable oil

1 cup coarsely chopped asparagus

1 teaspoon tamari or soy sauce

½ teaspoon finely grated orange or lemon zest

2½ cups cooked quinoa, brown rice, or millet

4 ounces cheddar cheese, coarsely grated (1 cup), divided

2–3 ounces (about ½ cup) crumbled feta cheese

½ cup chopped fresh parsley

4 eggs

½ teaspoon smoked or plain paprika

Salt and freshly ground pepper

1 Preheat the oven to 350°F. Lightly spray or brush a twelve-cup muffin tin with olive oil.

2 Heat the vegetable oil in a small skillet over medium-high heat and stir-fry the asparagus for about 5 minutes, until bright green and even a little browned in places. Remove from the heat and toss with the tamari and zest.

recipe continues

3 Combine the quinoa, ½ cup of the cheddar, feta, asparagus, parsley, and eggs in a medium bowl and mix well. Add the paprika, a fat pinch of salt, and a few twists of pepper.

4 Divide among the muffin cups and sprinkle the tops with the remaining ½ cup cheddar. Bake for about 20 minutes, until nicely golden brown, and then loosen the muffins with a quick trip around the edges with a butter knife or thin spatula so you can remove them to cool on a rack; they will sog a bit if left to cool in the pan.

5 Serve immediately, while hot, or at room temperature. These keep well in the refrigerator for 3 or 4 days, and will revive with a quick snap in a toaster oven. They can also be frozen for up to 3 months.

OTHER WAYS TO DO IT

- REPLACE THE ASPARAGUS WITH SHREDDED SPINACH, OR FINELY CHOPPED COOKED GREENS OF ANY TYPE.

- USING ALL CHEDDAR OR MONTEREY JACK CHEESE, REPLACE THE GREEN VEGETABLES WITH CUBED AND ROASTED SWEET POTATOES, DRAINED BLACK BEANS, AND A HANDFUL OF CHOPPED CILANTRO.

- SWAP THE CHEDDAR/FETA COMBINATION FOR MOZZARELLA, OR A SMOKY *SCAMORZA*, ADD A FEW CHOPPED ROASTED OR SUNDRIED TOMATOES ALONG WITH THE GREENS, AND REPLACE THE PARSLEY WITH FRESH BASIL.

- INCLUDE CRUMBLED BACON, SLIVERS OF HAM, COOKED SAUSAGE . . . OH, YOU GET THE IDEA.

STINK BUG EGGS

If there is a lover of hard-boiled eggs in your life who happens to have an eye for beauty or be under the age of ten, or both, this is a lunch-box ace in the hole. Roald Dahl's Revolting Recipes is a posthumously assembled collection of recipes for the foods that appear in Dahl's books and relies on the principle that a person of a certain age is more likely to eat a Stink Bug Egg than a hard-boiled egg, even though they are the same thing. It's a stupendous resource. This version of the eggs uses onion skins and black tea for the color that makes the patterns and delivers a mild hit of flavor with the color bath.

MAKES 6 EGGS

6 eggs

Pinch of baking soda

2 cups water

3 tablespoons tamari or soy sauce

2 tablespoons plain black tea leaves

Handful of onion skins

1 tablespoon finely chopped fresh ginger

1 Hard-boil your eggs by placing them in a saucepan with cold water to cover and a pinch of baking soda. Bring the water to a boil and maintain a simmer for 7 minutes. Remove the pan from the heat and let the eggs sit in the hot water, with the cover on, for another 7 minutes.

2 Transfer the eggs to a bowl of ice water. When they have cooled enough to handle, whap them lightly all over against the counter or with a spoon. You want the shell cracked but still intact.

3 Combine the water, tamari, tea leaves, onion skins, and ginger in the saucepan, and bring to a boil; cook for about 5 minutes, then let steep, covered, off the heat for about 1 hour.

recipe continues

4   Pour the brine, solids included, into a glass dish that you can cover securely. Nestle the eggs in the brine and let them sit at least overnight in the refrigerator or for up to 3 days before peeling.

OTHER WAYS TO DO IT

If eggs are a big hit with your packed-lunch crowd consider these tricks:

- ACHIEVE SOMETHING EXCITING AND COLORFUL BY NESTLING PEELED BOILED EGGS INTO PREPARED PURPLE SAUERKRAUT OR KIMCHI.

- QUAIL EGGS ARE OFTEN AVAILABLE IN ASIAN MARKETS OR FANCY SUPERMARKETS. HARD-BOILING THOSE IS A MATTER OF BRINGING THEM TO A BOIL WITH A PINCH OF BAKING SODA, AND ONCE THE WATER BOILS, TURNING OFF THE HEAT. LET THEM STAND IN THE HOT WATER, HEAT OFF AND POT COVERED, FOR 6 MINUTES. DRAIN THEM, THEN PLACE THEM IN A SMALL CONTAINER WITH A SECURE LID AND ½ CUP OF WATER. CLOSE THE CONTAINER AND SHAKE JUST HARD ENOUGH THAT THE SHELLS CRACK; PEEL AND PRESENT THEM FOR LUNCH TO CHEERS AND SIGHS.

- BOILED EGGS OF ANY BIRD, ESPECIALLY WHEN EITHER PICKLED OR VERY TINY, MAKE A BIG SPLASH WHEN TURNED INTO DEVILED EGGS. HALVE THE EGGS AND SCOOP ALL THE YOLKS INTO A SMALL BOWL. MASH THEM AND ADD (PER 6 CHICKEN EGGS): 1 TABLESPOON OF ANY TYPE OF PLAIN GREEK YOGURT, 1 TABLESPOON GOOD OLIVE OIL, 1 TEASPOON PREPARED MUSTARD OR *GOCHUJANG* CHILI PASTE, ½ TEASPOON MILD CURRY POWDER, AND 1 TABLESPOON OF MINCED FRESH BASIL, PARSLEY, OR SCALLION, OR A COMBINATION. MIX THOROUGHLY, THEN FILL HALF THE WAITING EGGS AND TOP WITH ANOTHER EGG HALF FOR EASY PACKING.

BAKED CUSTARD

with
CARAMEL

If baked custard is on your list of comfort foods, there is pretty much no other way to eat it than while making a quiet yummy sound. Aside from this happy truth, custard also contains a good amount of protein and calcium. Thanks to mason jars and their lids, this all adds up to a lunch-box winner. I like the tiny (4-ounce) mason jars that are sold for jelly, but you can use wide-mouth half-pint jars as well. This version has a few layers of flavor from the caramelized sugar and fresh herbs, but you can also do the custard very plainly, with nothing but sugar, milk, egg, and vanilla—or try one of the variations that follow the main recipe. As long as you pay attention to the timing (overbaking custard because I have let my mind wander makes me very crabby), you will make something pretty terrific.

SERVES 6 TO 8

¼–⅓ cup sugar

2 tablespoons water

2½ cups whole milk

1 sprig fresh mint or
basil

One 1-inch vanilla bean,
snipped open

4 eggs

¼ teaspoon sea salt

1 In a heavy saucepan, combine the sugar with the water. Heat without stirring over medium heat until the mixture comes to a low boil, and continue to cook for about 5 minutes, until it's a lovely deep amber. Immediately remove the pan from the heat, as it's a short hop from deep amber to deep trouble in the sugar-cooking world. Carefully pour in the milk, which may sputter so take precautions to protect your tender face, then add the mint and vanilla bean, and return to low heat. Stir until the now-hardened caramel melts and the mixture

recipe continues

returns to a simmer. Take the pot off the heat again, allowing about 10 minutes for the spices to steep and the milk to cool slightly.

2   During this time, preheat the oven to 325°F, and get six to eight 4-ounce mason jars ready by setting them in a pan that will hold the jars and enough hot water to climb halfway up the sides. Put the kettle on. Find a strainer and a pitcher.

3   Beat the eggs in a medium bowl along with the salt, and then pour in the infused milk, through a strainer to catch the spices. Whisk thoroughly.

4   Pour the egg and milk mixture back through the same strainer into the pitcher, to catch any eggy bits that would mar the smoothness of the custard. Divide the strained mixture among the waiting dishes, transfer the pan to the oven, and pour hot water from the kettle into the pan until it comes halfway up the sides of the jars.

5   Bake for about 25 minutes for 4-ounce jars or 35 minutes for larger ones, watching carefully at the end. For the silkiest texture, you want them just set (a little wiggle when you jiggle), not puffed or cracked or browned. They will continue cooking a bit after you remove them from the oven, so err on the underbaked side. Immediately after removing the pan from the oven, use tongs to transfer the cups to a cooling rack and cool to room temperature before securing the jar lids and refrigerating until cold.

6   Custards will keep for 1 week in the refrigerator.

OTHER WAYS TO DO IT

Once you fasten on to the notion that the milk can be infused with just about anything, and the kind of milk you use is not set in stone, and even the type of sweetener is open to consideration, ho-hum baked custard starts to look pretty glamorous. Try a pod of star anise in place of the mint, or a couple coins of ginger root, or a stick of cinnamon; use coconut or almond milk in place of some or all of the cow's milk, and have a look at maple syrup, honey, and coconut sugar as your sweeteners.

CHOCOLATE PUDDING

After my friend Kari tasted the second draft of this recipe, she thoughtfully gave me a set of eight pudding cups with snap-on lids to make it easier for me to keep bringing her pudding on the regular. Jam jars make a fine substitute if you live too far from Kari to get the same deal. You can use regular condensed milk in place of the condensed coconut milk called for here, but if aversion and not availability is the obstacle, even extremely coconut-averse people say this pudding does not taste remotely like coconut. All it brings is a super-silky, creamy texture. This recipe makes a lot of pudding, but I have never found that "made too much pudding" really amounts to a problem.

MAKES A GENEROUS 6 CUPS OF PUDDING, SERVING 8 TO 10 DEPENDING ON PORTION SIZE

½ cup natural or Dutch-process unsweetened cocoa powder

⅓ cup cornstarch

½ teaspoon salt

4 cups cow's milk or carton-type coconut milk

One 15-ounce can sweetened condensed coconut milk

4–6 ounces (170g) semisweet or bittersweet chocolate, chopped

1 teaspoon vanilla bean paste or vanilla extract

Whipped cream, to serve (optional)

1 Have ready eight to ten small dishes or mason jars.

2 Combine the cocoa, cornstarch, and salt in a heavy, medium saucepan. Slowly whisk in the fresh milk, then add the condensed milk and whisk together thoroughly.

3 Heat over a medium flame, stirring constantly with a wooden spoon and being sure to reach into all corners of the pot so no area scorches or remains unstirred. Bring it all the way to a low boil (only evident if you stop stirring, which you shouldn't do for long), and continue to cook for about 7 minutes, until the mixture is nicely thick and the waves from stirring stay visible on the surface. You'll also notice that a darker skin starts to form on the surface if an area stays undisturbed; that's another signal that it's done. Rest assured that the pudding will thicken considerably as it cools.

4   Remove the pot from the heat and add the chocolate, whisking until it is melted. Add the vanilla. At this point, you can ladle it into the waiting dishes, or continue whisking until the pudding has cooled, which yields a creamier texture and the ability to mound it up attractively in the dish. This can take some time; either put on a podcast or transfer the pudding to a stand mixer and set it to low.

5   Churned or not, let the dishes come to room temperature before covering and chilling them, or condensation will spoil their tidy tops.

6   Whipped cream makes a totally unnecessary but welcome embellishment. The pudding will keep for up to 1 week, refrigerated.

OTHER WAYS TO DO IT

You may be as surprised as I was to discover that the addition of ⅓ cup of canned pure pumpkin makes for an astonishingly silky texture, along with the extra nourishment it supplies. It is entirely undetectable in flavor terms.

PEACH TAPIOCA

Fruit tapioca is tasty and fast to make, and is so different from the creamy, egg-y way that tapioca usually gets treated that it will likely win over even any skeptics who may live in your house. I have no skeptics in my house. In my house I have to hide it in order to have enough for the lunch boxes the next day.

SERVES 4 TO 6

⅔ cup small pearl tapioca

¾ cup water

3 cups orange-carrot juice

2 cups coarsely chopped fresh or frozen peaches

¼–½ cup apple juice concentrate (sold in the frozen section), or 3 tablespoons honey or agave syrup

1 Put the tapioca and water in a medium saucepan to soak for about 30 minutes.

2 Add the orange-carrot juice, peaches, and apple juice concentrate; taste for sweetness and adjust as necessary.

3 Bring to a low boil, stirring all the while to prevent the tapioca from clumping to the bottom of the pot, and simmer for about 5 minutes, until a few of the tapioca balls test soft (they do not need to be clear, just tender).

4   Pour the pudding into a lidded container, or into a collection of small jars or bowls, and cool to room temperature before covering and chilling thoroughly. Tapioca will keep for up to 1 week in the refrigerator.

OTHER WAYS TO DO IT

You can substitute instant or minute tapioca for the small pearl, in which case you eliminate the soaking step and can whip it together even faster—just dump everything in the pot and cook. Everyone I feed loves peach, but the possible combinations of fruits and juices give a person myriad ways to mix it up.

FOUR SQUARES

A long time ago one of my children needed a math tutor, and thank goodness she did because in this way I opened the door to Alana Chernila one early evening in the fall of 2006. I can sort of remember what life was like before she was my friend, but it's pretty hazy. Among other reasons to love her, Alana is the queen of the Car Snack, a recipe for a granola bar-like item that she has published at least six versions of, all of them put forth so that the world could tinker with them to their own liking. I am not sure which version I started with anymore, but now I have a reliably repeatable rendition, which is cleared for takeoff even in our nut-free school. They have a good amount of fiber and protein in them even though they taste like a cookie, they hold up well to storing and mailing, and they can be varied in so many ways that no one ever really gets tired of them. All of this makes them an essential component of what I think of as the fourth square meal of the day, which is the one made up of snacks.

MAKES ONE 10 × 10 PAN OF SQUARES

½ cup (1 stick) unsalted butter or coconut oil
¾ cup thick, sticky sweetener, such as honey, Lyle's Golden Syrup, barley malt syrup, or rice syrup

2 tablespoons tahini or sunflower seed butter
¾ cup sunflower seeds
½ cup dried apricots, chopped
1 cup old-fashioned rolled oats

1 heaping cup puffed millet or crisp rice cereal (or you could use puffs of any grain)
¼ cup oat bran
¼ cup flax meal
½ teaspoon sea salt

1 Preheat the oven to 375°F. Ready a 10 × 10-inch baking pan, and line it with two pieces of parchment paper so that the bottom and sides of the pan are covered. Really. You may think you can just butter the pan but if you don't heed the warning about the parchment paper, you had better have a chisel handy.

2   Unwrap your stick of butter. Melt the butter and the honey together in a large pot, stirring all the while. Let it come to a nice boil over medium heat, cook for about 1 minute, then remove from the stove. Stir in the tahini and then the sunflower seeds, tossing to coat, and then stir in the apricots, oats, puffed millet, oat bran, flax meal, and salt.

3   Glop the mess onto the parchment in the pan. Use a spatula to pat it out as smoothly as you can.

4   Bake for about 20 minutes, until it is a lovely golden, toasty brown all over. Set the pan on a rack and let it cool for 5–10 minutes.

5   Let the bars cool to almost room temperature in the pan, then while they are still slightly warm, use the parchment to relocate the whole block onto a cutting surface. Using a large sharp knife, portion them out into squares, and store in an airtight container, or wrap individually in wax paper.

OTHER WAYS TO DO IT

Change up the fruits, seeds (or nuts), and grains to your taste as long as you keep to the approximate proportions. It's my duty to let you know that you can also pour half a bag of chocolate chips on top of these when they come out of the oven, and then once they melt, use an off-set spatula to smooth that out into a chocolate coating that will be firm enough to wrap once it cools.

SAVORY GRANOLA

Both care packages and granola have a tendency to get stuck at the sweet end of the spectrum. Great things happen when they are shoved to the other side. Savory Granola is tasty and nutritious eaten out of hand, and when people want to dress up plain rice, or salad, or whatever they are subsisting on off the tines of their spork, it brings some muscle to the project. Like all granolas, it is endlessly variable. Mix up the rolled grains or go all-coconut for a grain-less version. Switch out the nuts and seeds, vary the spices and seasonings—just keep the proportions of dry to liquid pretty constant and it all should come together into something you can slip into a cellophane bag and tie with a hipster-ish bit of twine.

MAKES ABOUT 3 CUPS

For the
BASE

½ cup old-fashioned
  rolled oats

½ cup unsweetened
  coconut ribbons

½ cup roasted cashews

½ cup sunflower seeds

½ cup shelled unsalted
  pistachios

¼ cup golden flax seeds

For the
GLUE

1 egg white (or 1
  tablespoon chia seed,
  bloomed for a few
  minutes in ¼ cup
  water)

¼ cup olive oil or
  coconut oil (or a blend
  of the two)

1–2 teaspoons maple
  syrup, agave, or
  coconut sugar

For the
SEASONING

2 teaspoons Preserved
  Lemon Puree (page 68)
  or tamari or soy sauce

½ teaspoon finely grated
  orange zest

2 teaspoons sesame oil

½ teaspoon toasted
  coriander seeds,
  crushed

½ teaspoon gochugaru
  (Korean ground red
  pepper) or paprika

1   Preheat the oven to 350°F. Line a rimmed baking sheet with parchment paper.

2   In a medium bowl, combine the oats, coconut, cashews, sunflower seeds, pistachios, and flax seeds. In a large bowl, combine the egg white, olive oil, and maple syrup with the preserved lemons, orange zest, sesame oil, coriander seeds, and gochugaru. Combine the two mixtures and toss well; taste and adjust the seasonings.

3   Spread the mixture out on the prepared baking sheet, and bake for about 25 minutes, stirring a few times to prevent scorching at the edges and get a nice even toastiness. Cool it, and store in an airtight jar for up to 1 month.

PRIORITY CHOCOLATE COOKIES

This is a cookie you want on your team. The cookies freeze well, both as cookies and at the balls-of-dough stage, so you can build a nice arsenal of them against future need, and they make dreamy little ice cream sandwiches if you go for that kind of thing. They are happy to travel, tolerating a Priority Mail ride with aplomb—their crispy edges, chewy centers, and general brownie-esque qualities weather transit like a boss.

MAKES 4 DOZEN COOKIES

For

GLUTEN-FREE COOKIES

1½ cup (135g) oat flour

1½ cups (240g) sweet
 rice flour

For

CONVENTIONAL COOKIES

Scant 3 cups (375g) all-
 purpose wheat flour

For

BOTH COOKIES

1¼ teaspoon baking
 soda

½ teaspoon salt

¾ cup (1½ sticks)
 unsalted butter

1½ cups (300g) lightly
 packed dark brown
 sugar

2 tablespoons brewed
 coffee

12 ounces (340g)
 semi- or bittersweet
 chocolate, chopped

¾ teaspoon vanilla
 extract

2 eggs

1 Whisk together your flour(s) of choice, baking soda, and salt in a medium bowl.

2 Heat the butter, sugar, and coffee in a medium to large saucepan over medium heat, stirring often, until the butter is melted and the mixture is bubbling at the edges. Remove from the heat. Add the chocolate and the vanilla, and stir until the chocolate is thoroughly melted and incorporated. Let the mixture stand to cool slightly, about 5 minutes.

3 With a wooden spoon and a vigorous stroke, stir the eggs into the chocolate mixture one at a time, stirring well after each. Slowly add the dry ingredients, in three or four additions, stirring until no visible streaks of flour remain, and then 10 strong strokes after that. The mixture will be soft, like brownie batter. Cover it snugly.

4 Refrigerate for at least an hour (and up to a day), until the mixture is thoroughly cool and has firmed. Do not skip this step!

5 Preheat the oven to 350°F, and line two baking sheets with parchment paper. Roll the cold dough into balls 1½ inches in diameter (you can freeze these for later, if you like), and place them 3–4 inches apart on the prepared baking sheet.

6 Bake for 9–11 minutes, until the tops have deep cracks and are just set to the touch. They will firm as they cool, so err on the side of underbaking to retain some chewiness. Use a thin spatula to remove the cookies to a rack to cool, then store airtight at room temperature, or they can be frozen for up to 3 months.

WING DINGS

These little cakes are proud descendants of Isa Chandra Moskowitz's Fauxstess Cupcakes, and if you don't know her vegan cookbooks, I suggest you remedy that ASAP: they are full of good food for all kinds of eaters, vegan or otherwise, and also a treasure trove of tips for making tasty things that don't contain things that people avoiding things may be avoiding, if that makes any sense. The thick chocolate on top here sets up solid, and the cupcake paper beneath keeps the underside fresh, which means that you can wrap them up and mail them and they do just fine in transit as long as you do not pick a sweltering week in August to do it. It's good to send them out because you are breeding joy that way, and it's also good to send them out because it's very dangerous to try to share a household with a full batch of them. Black cocoa, which is readily available at baking supply places, makes these extra special, but you can use an equivalent amount of regular baking cocoa in its place.

MAKES 24 LITTLE CAKES

For
GLUTEN-FREE WING DINGS

½ cup (55g) sweet rice flour

½ cup (55g) oat flour

¼ cup (25g) coconut flour

½ cup (60g) tapioca flour

2 tablespoons (14g) cornstarch

For
CONVENTIONAL WING DINGS

1⅔ cups (215g) all-purpose wheat flour

For
BOTH WING DINGS

⅓ cup milk (plant or dairy)

2 teaspoons white or apple cider vinegar

1 tablespoon flax meal

2 tablespoons water

½ cup (44g) natural (not Dutch-process) cocoa powder

¼ cup (22g) black cocoa powder

1 teaspoon baking powder

½ teaspoon baking soda

½ teaspoon salt

½ cup vegetable shortening

1 cup sugar

1 teaspoon vanilla extract

½ cup + 1 tablespoon near-boiling water

For the
WHITE FILLING

¾ cups Whuff (page 152) or Marshmallow Fluff (see headnote, page 150)

½ cup vegetable shortening, at cool room temperature

¼ teaspoon salt

½ teaspoon vanilla bean paste or vanilla extract

1 teaspoon cream or non-dairy creamer

For the
CHOCOLATE TOP

4 ounces (115g) semisweet chocolate, chopped, divided

1 tablespoon coconut oil

1   Preheat the oven to 350°F, and line eighteen muffin cups with paper liners.

2   Combine the milk and vinegar in a small bowl. In another small bowl, combine the flax meal and the 2 tablespoons of water. Leave these to rest while you prepare the other ingredients.

3   Sift the flour(s), cocoa powder, black cocoa powder, baking powder, baking soda, and salt together into a medium bowl.

4   In another bowl, cream the shortening, and then add the sugar and beat for 2–3 minutes.

5   Add the flax mixture to this bowl, and cream it well.

6   Now add a third of the dry ingredients, and beat to combine. Add the soured milk, along with the vanilla extract, and beat at low speed until smooth. Add half the remaining dry ingredients, and beat well. Slowly add ½ cup of the very hot water, beating at low speed to combine, and then scrape the bowl once and add the remaining dry

recipe continues

ingredients; beat on low until smooth. Add the remaining tablespoon of hot water and beat at low speed to incorporate, raising the speed to medium for the last 15 seconds to aerate the batter.

7 Portion into the cupcake pan, filling the cups no more than half full (a #40 scoop works well for even portioning). Bake for 12–16 minutes, until the tops spring back, and remove the little cakes to a rack to cool.

8 While the cakes cook and cool, prepare the filling and chocolate top.

9 To make the filling, put the Whuff, shortening, salt, and vanilla bean paste in the bowl of the mixer and beat at medium-high speed until smoothly combined. Drizzle in the cream, beating constantly. Set aside.

10 To make the topping, place about 3 ounces of the chocolate and the coconut oil in a heatproof spouted measuring cup, and set it into a pan of water set over medium-low heat until the chocolate begins to melt.

11 Remove the pan from the heat but leave the setup as is, allowing the residual heat of the water to gently melt the chocolate as you stir.

12 When it is completely melted, remove the cup from the water and add the remaining 1 ounce chocolate, stirring until the mixture is smooth; this speeds the cooling and helps to temper the chocolate.

13 Leave at room temperature; you want a not-hot but still-liquid glaze for the little cakes.

14 Now it's time to put it all together. Once the cakes are completely cool, fill a pastry bag fitted with a plain tube tip (for which you can substitute a plastic bag with one corner cut off to create a ½-inch opening) with the filling.

15 Poink the metal tip into the center of the cupcake (if your setup has no metal tip, you will need to use something like the handle of a spoon to create a pilot hole) and give a gentle squeeze on the bag; the cupcake will puff up slightly as its belly gets filled. Continue the poink-and-puff maneuver until all the cakes are filled. Use a tiny spoon to level any filling sticking up higher than the surface of the cupcake.

16 Pour the cool but still runny chocolate over the tops, letting it pool to the edges of the cupcake papers. Repeat for each cake, then set aside at cool room temperature or in the fridge to solidify. Once set, the frosting will be firm even at room temperature. These are fine at room (or post-office) temperature for a few days. They will stay fresher in the fridge, for up to 1 week, but are best eaten at room temperature.

OTHER WAYS TO DO IT

- IF YOU ARE MORE IN THE MARKET FOR A WHOOPIE PIE, USE A PARCHMENT-LINED BAKING SHEET RATHER THAN A MUFFIN PAN. USE A #40 (1.75 OUNCE) SPRING-LOADED SCOOP TO PORTION THE DOUGH OUT, 3 INCHES APART, AND BAKE FOR 9–10 MINUTES, UNTIL THE TOPS SPRING BACK. LET COOL 5 MINUTES ON THE BAKING SHEET, THEN USE A WIDE, FLEXIBLE SPATULA TO TRANSFER THE COOKIES TO A RACK TO COOL COMPLETELY. DOUBLE THE FILLING RECIPE, AND USE A GENEROUS SPOONFUL OF THE WHITE FILLING TO SANDWICH THE COOKIES TOGETHER, FOREGOING THE CHOCOLATE COATING.

- IF IT IS A FUNNY BONE YOU AIM TO RECONNECT WITH, REPLACE HALF OF THE VEGETABLE SHORTENING IN THE FILLING WITH SMOOTH NO-STIR PEANUT BUTTER.

A HELL OF A COOKIE, ALL THINGS CONSIDERED

These are the undercover agents of the cookie world. If you have to please a lot of people of divergent diets with one dessert, my feeling is usually to splurge on a nice fruit bowl or bake some apples. But it's a little bit of a superpower to have up your sleeve a cookie that can satisfy many different diets and still walk proudly as a bona fide treat. This is that cookie. They are simple to make, friendly to a long list of requirements, stand up well to transport, and can be easily modified to suit fancier occasions.

MAKES 2 TO 3 DOZEN COOKIES

1 cup (160g) sweet rice flour

1 cup (200g) almond meal or almond flour

½ cup (60g) sugar

¼ cup golden flax meal

½ teaspoon Maldon or other flaky salt

Finely grated zest of ½ lemon

6 tablespoons unsalted butter, cut into 1-inch pieces

3.5 ounces (half a tube) almond paste, cut into 1-inch pieces

2 tablespoons excellent olive oil

1 tablespoon honey

1 teaspoon vanilla extract

1   Combine the rice flour, almond meal, sugar, flax meal, salt, and lemon zest in the bowl of a food processor and pulse to combine. Add the butter, almond paste, olive oil, honey, and vanilla, and pulse until finely incorporated. Now let the machine run for about 30 seconds to 1 minute, until the dough gathers together.

2   On a sheet of wax paper, pat the dough into a log and chill until firm, about 10 minutes in the freezer or about an hour in the fridge.

You can also freeze the log of dough for later use. I have baked them straight from frozen, and the results were indistinguishable.

3 Preheat the oven to 325°F, and line a baking sheet with parchment paper. Slice the cookies ¼-inch thick and arrange them on the sheet (they barely spread at all). Bake for about 8 minutes, until just golden on the edges, and let them cool on the parchment for a few minutes before moving them to a rack. They are perilously soft when first baked, but nice and sturdy once they cool.

OTHER WAYS TO DO IT

- IF YOU WANT SOMETHING A LITTLE FLASHIER, PULSE IN ⅓ CUP OF DRIED CHERRIES OR CRANBERRIES WITH THE OTHER INGREDIENTS IN THE FIRST STEP. SWAP ORANGE ZEST FOR THE LEMON ZEST IF YOU GO THIS ROUTE.

- MELT 2–4 OUNCES OF BITTERSWEET CHOCOLATE AND TAKE THE COOKIES FOR A HALF-DIP OR DRIZZLE IT ON TOP.

GOLDEN MILK TO GO

This wellness formula is the absolute ticket to soothe jangled exam-time nerves and convey the essence of care and company to someone who's out of reach. Turmeric is a potent anti-inflammatory, soothing aches and pains as well as nerves, and a small kick of black pepper aids the body in absorbing the full benefits of the other spices. Golden milk isn't very difficult for people to make if they have all the spices on hand, but then again, lots of things are both not difficult and good for us, and yet we rarely do them for ourselves, even if someone sends us an article. Creating this ready-to-use mix makes it basically instant gratification for the recipient, no more difficult to prepare on their end than chalky cocoa from a packet and so much better for everyone and everything. In these proportions the resulting blend of flavors is pretty low-key; increase the ginger to give it more oomph, and add more sugar (or send it with a squeeze bear of honey) if your recipient has a sweet tooth. Coconut milk powder is commonly available in big health food stores and supermarkets, and all Asian groceries.

MAKES ABOUT 1 CUP OF MIX

For the
GOLDEN MILK MIX

¼ cup ground turmeric

¾ cup coconut milk
  powder

2 tablespoons coconut
  sugar

¼ teaspoon freshly
  ground pepper

1 teaspoon ground
  cinnamon

2 tablespoons ground
  ginger

¼ teaspoon sea salt

For
ONE SERVING

1–2 teaspoons Golden
  Milk Mix

¾ cup milk (plant or
  dairy) or water

1 teaspoon ghee
  (optional)

1 Combine the turmeric, coconut milk powder, sugar, pepper, cinnamon, ginger, and salt in a small bowl and whisk thoroughly, until completely combined and free of lumps, bumps, and clumps. Store in a glass jar with a tight-fitting lid.

2   To use, whisk 1–2 teaspoons of the mix into ¾ cup of hot milk, whisking until smooth. This is excellent foamed, as a latte or cappuccino might be; you can also mix it into hot water, then add a dollop of milk, cream, or steamed milk to finish.

3   A teaspoon of ghee sends this concoction off the top end of the delicious gauge. A little jar of ghee, a honey bear, and this mix makes a pretty handsome gift.

7

FOOD FOR A CROWD

THE SHARING OF FOOD
IS THE BASIS OF
SOCIAL LIFE,
and to many people it is the
ONLY KIND
OF SOCIAL LIFE WORTH
PARTICIPATING IN

LAURIE COLWIN,
Home Cooking

I HAVE TO ADMIT THAT AT THE OPENING-DAY PICNIC AT MY KIDS' FORMER SCHOOL, I WAS AMONG THE PEOPLE WHO WERE DODGING THE FRIENDLY MOM WITH THE CLIPBOARD WHO WAS SEEKING OUT PARENTS TO COOK SOUP FOR THE FACULTY AND STAFF FOR THE THURSDAY STAFF MEETING. HER JOB WAS NOT AN EASY ONE. SHE HAD A SCHEDULE FOR THE YEAR AND SHE NEEDED TO POPULATE IT WITH PEOPLE WHO FELT WILLING TO MAKE AND (AS I LATER LEARNED WAS A SIGNIFICANT PART OF THE CHALLENGE) *TRANSPORT* SOUP FOR FORTY EATERS FROM THEIR HOME KITCHEN TO THE SCHOOL BREAKROOM. IT WAS HARD TO SAY "I DON'T HAVE TIME!" TO THIS MOM OF FOUR SCHOOL-AGE CHILDREN WHO RAN HER OWN BUSINESS AND WAS ALSO PRESIDENT OF THE PTA. WHEN SHE COLLARED ME, AND I EXPRESSED MY TREPIDATION ABOUT MAKING THAT MUCH SOUP, SHE WAVED IT OFF. SHE TOLD ME THAT IT WAS NOT A BIG DEAL AT ALL FOR HER, AND SHE WAS SURE I WOULD FIND THE SAME TO BE TRUE FOR ME. "YOU LOVE TO COOK!" SHE SAID.

A s it happens, though, a fondness for cooking and even experience catering little dinner parties, which I had, only carry you so far when you are talking about feeding a big crowd. They call on related muscle groups, but cooking for a multitude is definitely a whole other sport. My father, who spent a total of one semester in hotel school before sparing himself and that industry with a career change, *says* he knows how to make soup for 250 people, but that assertion is untested in my lifetime, and he never even shared his notes with me.

There ended up being a good amount of soup in the floor mats of my car (I know a lot more now than I once did about the physics of sloshing and the relative seal of various types of lids) but I did manage to make a large amount of a tasty soup, which of course earned me (among other things) the right and responsibility at the next fall's picnic to come out early from my hidey-hole behind the swing set and take my pick of dates on her still-blank sign-up sheet, and so on through the years until we switched schools for what I promise are entirely unrelated reasons.

Not long ago, I started cooking community supper at the local community center where I live. I had been pretty interested in being part of this kind of endeavor for a while. On November 9, 2016, like many others I was casting around for something constructive to do before I lost the last vestiges of hope for the future of kindness and possibility. It seemed threatened then and there's little in the time since, not to mention the forecast, to suggest that pressure will lift. The community center serves a meal every Monday night to a diverse group that includes seniors, thru-hikers on the Appalachian Trail, residents and caregivers from local group homes for special-needs adults, people of all ages and backgrounds who live alone and welcome the company, and a sprinkling of people—often couples or families—who like to exit their comfort zones and find out what life is like for others where we live. Basically you see people of all stripes eating together at one table, just like I was taught that America is supposed to be. My thinking went something like this: It's hard to share food with people you hate, but it's also hard to hate people you share food with. Get more people sharing food. Crowd out the hatred. Fill people up with each other's goodness and they will have no room for false assumptions and bad intentions. There isn't much leeway anymore to opt out of activism. I am nervous in crowds and unlikely to run for office, but feeding people is in my muscle memory as well as my philosophical wheelhouse, and those are good foundations for an action plan.

Getting a hot entree and all its accompaniments ready at the same time, at that scale (about 120 people attend these dinners, on average), with unfamiliar equipment, on a firm deadline—well, that is the kind of circumstance that anxiety dreams eat for breakfast, to fortify themselves for the night ahead. If you are interested in doing this kind of thing as well, take heed of the following: Don't fuss too much about your level of experience even if you have never cooked for more than a handful of people. You will be well served if you have a sense of what kinds of things taste good together, and some familiarity with the techniques and ingredients involved in preparing them, and so forth, but willingness to do things and be helped by others are just as important. If you have the latter and not the former, I think you can still win at this and I definitely think it is worth trying.

Another thing I can tell you that might be relaxing is that I learned quickly to check my devotion to scratch cooking, already put to the test during the soup affair. Bringing that soup up to the required level in the tank involved some panicked eleventh-hour (like, literally at 11:00 p.m.) lobbing of canned chickpeas and other convenience foods into the pot to bulk things up. Because here's the thing: most people cooking on a large scale rely on one or more of the following: a team of prep cooks, a lot of hours, or a food service company that will sell them already-prepared ingredients in big containers.

Fortunately, I set out on this adventure not only to serve people good food, but to work with people who were doing good, and I was lucky enough to fall in among a lovely group of kitchen-dwellers, making help easy to source. Using things in cans and jars (those chickpeas, for example, or prepared salsa) helps me make meal prep fit into one day, and consequently into my life with my family, and that trade-off is worth it for me, especially if I can source the items responsibly.

Like most people, the diners at the community center see a lot of pasta, and for good reason: it is pretty hard to botch things like baked ziti and chili-mac, and they are easy to produce on the cheap. A baked pasta, and maybe some sheet pans of quartered roasted apples to serve with ice cream, are fantastically simple places to start your multiplication table adventure. The recipes here give you options to expand your repertoire, and are written in quantities to feed twenty people, which I hope makes for simple math and spans a variety of needs: from showing up for the staff of the crisis center through having dinner ready for a local chapter meeting of whichever cause you're putting your muscle into, and all the way to taking part in serving a big mixer of a community meal where you live. They're useful for big potlucks too, and (when divvied into suitable containers) for loading a freezer with meals you can draw on when a group of any size pops across your radar appearing unable to meet the challenge of getting itself fed.

NOT EXACTLY SCONES

This recipe came originally from The Kripalu Cookbook, a volume that I used so hard in my children's youth that the binding has disintegrated. There is no way to calculate how many times and how many different ways I made these scones, or how many playdates and meetings and potlucks they went off to, or the countless morphs and tweaks that have taken place since I first cracked the spine of that book. The "recipe" has an elastic ability to accommodate whatever lurks in your pantry (this is why it looks long, because of all the possible substitutions), combines all manner of nutritious items into one convenient handheld snack, and is almost universally enjoyed because—hallelujah—it tastes like dessert. One recipe yields a mondo batch. Be aware that you can bake one tray all the way to done and deploy it immediately, and you can underbake the other tray, freeze it, and haul it out at a later date when time is short and you wish you had time to bake something. Just defrost them overnight in the fridge and give them a final snap in the oven in the morning. You can also mix all the dry ingredients at night, just before stumbling to bed, and come daybreak find that you are halfway to Scone Town.

MAKES 16 LARGE SCONES OR ABOUT 24 SMALL SCONES

For
GLUTEN-FREE SCONES

2 cups (230g) sweet
   rice flour
1 cup (100g) oat flour
½ cup (70g) buckwheat
   flour

For
CONVENTIONAL SCONES

4 cups (400g) whole
   wheat pastry flour

For
BOTH SCONES

1½ cups (170g) old-
   fashioned rolled oats
½ cup (60g) sugar
¼ cup (50g) almond
   meal or flour
½ cup (50g) oat bran

1 tablespoon baking
   powder
1 teaspoon baking soda
½ teaspoon ground
   cardamom
½ teaspoon salt
1½ cups buttermilk
1 teaspoon vanilla
¾ cup (1½ sticks)
   unsalted butter,
   melted

For the
FLAVOR ELEMENTS

1 cup chopped toasted
  almonds
1 cup chopped fresh
  or frozen peaches, in
  ½-inch pieces

½ cup frozen
  raspberries, smashed
½ cup golden raisins
2 tablespoons minced
  crystallized ginger

1   Preheat the oven to 375°F, and line two baking sheets with parchment paper.

2   Combine the flour(s), oats, sugar, almond meal, oat bran, baking powder, baking soda, cardamom, and salt in a large bowl. Add the buttermilk and vanilla and stir a few times, then add the butter. Stir twice, then toss in your flavor elements—the almonds, peaches, raspberries, raisins, and ginger—and continue to mix until all is just combined. Aim for a mixture that is uniformly moist but not wet, more dough than batter, in clumps that hold together when pressed.

3   Divide the dough into two portions for large scones, or into thirds for small ones. Place each onto a lined baking sheet. Gently pat the dough into a circle about 1 inch thick, keeping the edges rough.

4   Brush the top of each circle with butter and sprinkle the sugar on top. Using a bench knife or large kitchen knife, cut the circle in half, pushing the halves about ½ inch apart with the blade, and then in quarters, repeating the shove-apart maneuver, and then cut each quarter in half again, giving a little nudge, until you have eight triangles in a kind of blown-apart circle. Repeat for the other circle(s) of dough.

recipe continues

5 You can also make these as drop scones, especially if your mixture is wetter than predicted. Glob about ¾ cup per scone onto the cookie sheets with a little space between, drizzling the tops with melted butter and a sprinkle of sugar.

6 Bake for 20 minutes, until golden brown, reversing the trays halfway through.

OTHER WAYS TO DO IT

As the headnote explains, these scones are love substitutions. Here are some ways you can customize the recipe.

- FOR SUGAR, USE SUCANAT, DATE SUGAR, COCONUT SUGAR, OR BROWN SUGAR.

- FOR ALMOND FLOUR, USE PECAN MEAL; FOR A NUT-FREE VERSION, CHOOSE HEMP HEARTS OR FLAX MEAL, OR INCREASE THE OAT BRAN.

- FOR BUTTERMILK, USE SOY MILK OR NUT MILK, SOURED WITH 2 TEASPOONS OF WHITE OR APPLE CIDER VINEGAR OR LEMON JUICE, OR ANY TYPE OF YOGURT THINNED WITH MILK.

- FOR BUTTER, USE GHEE OR COCONUT OIL.

- FOR ALMONDS, USE ANY CHOPPED NUT OR TOASTED, WHOLE SEED, OR FLAKED COCONUT.

- FOR THE RAISINS, USE ANY CHOPPED DRIED FRUIT SUCH AS APRICOTS, APPLES, MANGO, OR WHOLE DRIED CHERRIES OR CRANBERRIES.

- FOR THE PEACHES AND RASPBERRIES, USE FROZEN OR FRESH BERRIES, OR APPLE, PEAR, OR MANGO.

GREAT BIG ENCHILADA-ISH BAKE

When my sisters and I were wrangling a collection of little cousins whom we often fed together, I stumbled across a recipe for Chilaquile Casserole in Mollie Katzen's Still Life With Menu Cookbook. It was delicious and nourishing and totally simple to make and we abused the privilege of its discovery so severely that my oldest nephew re-christened the dish "Chili-Kill-Me Casserole." Its simplicity and flexibility came to mind when trying to think of ways to make a huge dinner, as it accommodates whatever you have access to or is on sale at the grocery store (roast chicken, for example, can sub in for the ground meat) and whomever is expected for dinner (for vegetarians, you can leave the meat out entirely), has subtasks that are easily delegated to helping hands, and is content to be made ahead or held at temperature for a while. Cheese is basically the most expensive of the ingredients here, and even without especially savvy preordering in bulk (which my local markets happily allow, definitely bringing the cost way down), I am able to make this and a side vegetable for 140 people for under $200, which is not too shabby.

SERVES 20

For the
BASIC ENCHILADA

Vegetable oil, for
  greasing
10 cups Enchilada
  Sauce (recipe follows)
  or prepared salsa,
  divided
6 cups buttermilk
9 eggs

36 corn tortillas
2 pounds Monterey
  Jack or mild cheddar
  cheese, coarsely
  grated (8 cups),
  divided
One 10- to 12-ounce
  package tortilla chips

For the
FILLING

2 cups cooked, drained
  pinto or black beans
  (one 25-ounce can,
  drained)
2 pounds ground beef
  or turkey, browned
1 tablespoon ground
  cumin

recipe continues

One 12-ounce package
frozen corn kernels
Two 4-ounce cans
chopped roasted
green chilies

One 7-ounce jar salad
olives (green olives
and pimientos),
drained and coarsely
chopped
4 cups cubed potatoes
(about 1.5 pounds),

boiled to just tender
and drained
1 bunch fresh cilantro,
chopped (about
1 cup)

1 Lightly oil two 9 × 13 × 2½-inch baking/lasagna pans. Put 1 cup of sauce in the bottom of each pan.

2 Beat the buttermilk and eggs together in a spouted bowl and set aside.

3 Now turn toward the filling. Combine the beans, meat, cumin, corn, chilies, olives, potatoes, and cilantro in a large bowl and toss together thoroughly. Thanks to the olives, this shouldn't need much salt (and be mindful that more is coming from the cheese) but double-check with a quick taste.

4 Divide the tortillas in two equal stacks, and cut each stack in half. In a fun spatial alignment exercise that need not be very precise, use one of these four piles to create a more or less even layer of tortillas that goes all the way to the edges of the first pan. You'll quickly figure it out, but it pays to start with a ring of pieces with their straight sides to the edges of the pan, then fill in from there. Repeat with another pile on the second pan.

5 Distribute 3 cups of the filling mixture over the tortilla layer, then 2 cups of the sauce. Sprinkle 2 cups of the cheese over that. Repeat for the second pan.

6 Create another tortilla layer in each pan, finishing those off, and divide the remaining filling between the two pans. Add 2 cups of sauce to each pan, and sprinkle 1 cup of cheese over each.

7 Pour the buttermilk mixture gently over the top, dividing it evenly between the two pans. At three or four spots around the perimeter of the dish, insert a flexible spatula along the side of the pan to allow the buttermilk to seep down a bit.

8 Bash the bag of chips up, crumbling them inside the bag. Add the remaining 2 cups of cheese to the bag and shake to combine. Distribute this mixture on top of the two pans and let stand about 20 minutes before baking. You can also pause the whole process here for a few hours if you want to bake it later; just put it in the fridge and let it come to room temp before you bake it, uncovered, at 375°F for about 50 minutes, until golden on top and a quick poke near the center shows that the custard is set. Cooked, this will keep for 3–5 days refrigerated or up to 3 months frozen.

OTHER WAYS TO DO IT

You need 12 cups of filling to make the two pans. There's room for quite a lot of variation as you build it up:

- FOR A VEGETARIAN VERSION, SUBSTITUTE ANOTHER 2 CUPS OF BEANS FOR THE BROWNED MEAT, OR OPT FOR SAUTÉED ZUCCHINI OR CUBED, COOKED POTATOES (YUKON GOLD OR YAMS).

- FOR AN ALTERNATIVE MEATY VERSION, SUBSTITUTE SHREDDED ROAST CHICKEN OR CHOPPED CHORIZO SAUSAGE.

ENCHILADA SAUCE

A few chipotles in adobo, minced and added with the tomatoes, make a nice addition to the flavors in the sauce, if you know your diners are amenable to a little heat.

MAKES ABOUT 12 CUPS

½ cup olive oil

3 large yellow onions, about 2½ pounds, finely chopped

1 medium head of garlic (about 3 ounces), minced

2 tablespoons ground cumin

3 tablespoons ancho chili powder

One 4-ounce can tomato paste

One 28-ounce can fire-roasted ground or chopped tomatoes

1 cup brewed coffee

2 tablespoons lime juice

2 tablespoons maple syrup

2⅓ cups broth (chicken or vegetable), or water

½–1 tablespoon salt

1 bunch fresh cilantro, washed and finely chopped (about 1 cup)

1 Heat the oil in a large skillet over medium heat and sauté the onions for about 15 minutes, until they are soft and just beginning to brown.

2 Add the garlic, cumin, and chili powder, stir a time or two, and then add the tomato paste, stirring until it's blended before adding the tomatoes, coffee, lime juice, maple syrup, and broth. Let this come to a simmer and cook for about 10 minutes, until fragrant.

3 Stir in ½ tablespoon of salt, and then the cilantro. Taste for a balance of flavors, adding as much of the remaining ½ tablespoon salt as you like.

4 Use immediately, or cool and refrigerate for up to 4 days. The sauce can also be frozen for up to 3 months.

OTHER WAYS TO DO IT

With the addition of 1–2 pounds of browned turkey or beef and a 25-ounce can of kidney, pinto, or black beans, drained, this becomes enough to sauce 6 pounds of cooked, drained elbow macaroni; spread that mixture in a baking pan, liberally sprinkle the surface with grated cheddar or Jack cheese and crumbled tortilla chips, and bake for about 20 minutes, until toasty on top, and you have brought chili-mac to life.

A CAULDRON OF SOUP

This is a mildly Moroccan soup that scales up easily and, with a few tweaks (see the suggestions below the recipe), can be steered through an entirely different section of the world atlas for the next gathering. For any purpose, roasting cauliflower (or other brassicas) until lightly caramelized eliminates any cabbage-y qualities and here adds a nice layer of flavor to the soup.

SERVES 20

½ cup olive oil

2 large yellow onions (about 2 pounds), finely chopped

1 medium head of garlic (about 2 ounces), minced

2 teaspoons salt

6 cups cooked chickpeas (two 25-ounce cans, drained)

1 tablespoon ground cumin

2 teaspoons sweet or plain paprika

Four 28-ounce cans plain whole plum tomatoes

12 cups broth (chicken or vegetable), or water

6 additional cups water

1 cup pearled barley (or short-grain brown rice, if gluten is an issue)

2 large bunches kale (about 2 pounds), tough center stems removed, washed and finely sliced, or two 10-ounce packages frozen

For the
ROASTED VEGETABLES

1 large head cauliflower (about 2 pounds)

3 pounds carrots

½ cup olive oil

2 teaspoons kosher salt

¼ teaspoon ground cinnamon

½ teaspoon freshly ground pepper

1 teaspoon turmeric powder

1 teaspoon dried thyme leaves

Finely grated zest and juice of 1 large lemon

1 Heat the oil over medium heat in an 8-gallon stockpot and add the onions and garlic. Reduce the heat to low, add the salt, and sauté for about 15 minutes or until the onions are quite soft.

2 Meanwhile, coarsely grind the chickpeas with just a few pulses in a food processor, or mash them with a potato masher until they are pretty thoroughly broken up but not pureed. Add the cumin and paprika to the onion mixture, stir once, then add the chickpeas and continue to sauté for another 5 minutes. Break up the tomatoes a little, either with a few pulses in the same food processor bowl or just with your hands, and add these along with the broth, water, and barley. Return to a low boil and then reduce the heat to achieve a low simmer.

3 Heat the oven to 425°F. Trim the leaves and thick base from the cauliflower and break it apart into tiny florets. Peel the carrots, halve and then quarter them lengthwise, and chop them into ½-inch pieces. In a large bowl, toss the carrots and cauliflower with the oil and seasonings and spread them on two baking sheets in a single layer. Roast for 20–25 minutes, reversing the pans and tossing the vegetables at least once during that time, or until tender and lightly caramelized.

4 When the barley is tender, add the kale to the pot, and once it softens, the roasted vegetables. Add the lemon juice to the pot before tasting and adjust the salt as needed.

5 This soup can be used immediately, refrigerated for up to a week, or frozen for up to 3 months. The grain thickens things up as the soup gets reheated, so you may need to thin it with additional water or broth as you go along.

recipe continues

OTHER WAYS TO DO IT

- FOR A MORE MEDITERRANEAN EXPERIENCE, WHERE IT SAYS CHICKPEAS, USE WHITE BEANS (YOU CAN EASILY MASH THESE WITHOUT A FOOD PROCESSOR) AND OMIT THE CUMIN. WHEN YOU ROAST THE VEGETABLES, KEEP THE THYME AND LEMON AS IS BUT SWAP OUT THE CINNAMON AND TURMERIC FOR A TEASPOON OF OREGANO. EXCHANGE SLIVERED FULL-LEAF SPINACH (NOT BABY SPINACH) FOR THE KALE. ABOUT A CUP OF FINELY CHOPPED KALAMATA OR GREEN OLIVES (OR ½ CUP OLIVE PASTE) STIRRED IN AT THE END MAKES THIS VERSION EXTRA MEMORABLE.

- YOU CAN ADD BULK TO THE SOUP POT ECONOMICALLY (AND DELICIOUSLY) BY INCLUDING DICED YUKON GOLD OR WHITE POTATOES; JUST INCREASE THE WATER OR BROTH BY A CUP PER MEDIUM POTATO. POTATOES ARE NOTORIOUS FOR ABSORBING SALT IN A SOUP (SO MUCH SO THAT THEY ARE A GREAT WAY TO CORRECT AN OVERSALTED ONE), SO INCREASE THE SALT ACCORDINGLY.

PUMPKIN BREAD PUDDING

People at the community supper do not tend to appreciate bold and novel food. They like familiar ingredients, recognizable presentations, and comforting flavors. Even if the crowd you are feeding is more adventurous in appetite, as the cook you're likely to appreciate a dessert that comes together with very little effort. This bread pudding rings a lot of the same bells as pumpkin pie with about a tenth of the fuss per serving, and it's an excellent alchemy to perform on a windfall of day-old bread. It's delicious under a dollop of the sweet/tangy whipped cream described below but equally content with vanilla ice cream to, you know, cut the richness. Pumpkin seeds (only mildly adventurous) make an excellent stand-in for the pecans if you are cooking for a nut-free audience. A mixture of a tender bread like challah with something sturdier, such as a baguette, makes a nice balance but whatever bread you have to work with, the pumpkin potion will transform it into something delicious.

SERVES 20 TO 30

2 tablespoons unsalted butter, for greasing the pans

6 cups half-and-half

One 29-ounce + one 15-ounce can pure pumpkin

3 packed cups dark brown sugar

6 eggs

1 tablespoon + 1 teaspoon ground cinnamon

3 teaspoons ground ginger

¾ teaspoon ground nutmeg

¾ teaspoon salt

2 teaspoons vanilla extract

2½ pounds bread, a mixture of challah or other egg bread and baguette, cut or torn into 1–2 inch pieces

1½ cups dried cranberries

For the
TOPPING

6 ounces pecans, finely chopped

6 tablespoons unsalted butter

½ packed cup dark brown sugar

¾ teaspoon kosher salt

Freshly ground pepper

recipe continues

For the **WHIPPED CREAM**	1 cup sour cream or crème fraîche	3 tablespoons powdered sugar, sifted
2 cups heavy cream	1 teaspoon vanilla extract	

1   Preheat the oven to 350°F and generously butter two 9 × 13 × 2-inch cake pans.

2   In a large bowl, whisk together the half-and-half, pumpkin, dark brown sugar, eggs, spices, salt, and vanilla extract.

3   Using a large, flexible spatula, fold in the bread cubes and then the cranberries. Transfer the mixture to the prepared baking dishes.

4   In a skillet set over medium heat, toast the pecan pieces until lightly colored and fragrant. Remove to a bowl. Add the butter to the skillet and, once it melts, add the brown sugar, salt, and pepper. Cook, stirring, until the sugar melts. Remove from the heat and add the nuts, stirring to coat.

5   Divide the caramel nuts between the two pans, sprinkling the surface with them.

6   Bake the bread pudding until a tester inserted into the center comes out clean, about 40 minutes. Serve warm. This can be baked ahead and placed in a slow (300°F) oven to warm through before serving. It will keep 3–5 days refrigerated and up to a month frozen.

7   While the bread pudding bakes, beat the heavy cream and sour cream together with the vanilla and sugar until soft peaks form, and chill this mixture until the bread pudding is ready to serve.

CARING FOR
THE CAREGIVER

SO IT HAPPENS THAT WHEN I WRITE OF HUNGER I am really writing about LOVE AND THE HUNGER FOR IT, and warmth and the love of it and the hunger for it . . . and then the WARMTH AND RICHNESS AND FINE REALITY OF HUNGER SATISFIED . . . AND IT IS ALL ONE.

M. F. K. FISHER, *The Art of Eating*

During my sister's illness, I had a couple of occasions to find myself alone with her in a hotel in a strange city. When she was at home, my sister was surrounded by enough support that it was possible for those of us in her circle to take turns being with her. While traveling in search of treatment, care was provided by one person at a time, in twenty-four-hour shifts on cycles of about a week, until the next person could materialize and take over. I've rarely felt as tired or bereft as I did in that faraway city where I didn't speak the language, knew not one single soul, and where the relief of the familiar was too far away or off-kilter on the clock to make contact with, and the worry and the hours on duty seemed to never cease. I never felt old enough to be in charge of what I was in charge of; I was perpetually looking over my shoulder for the grown-up who ought to be handling things.

Midway through the first trip, I discovered there was a swimming pool in the basement of the hotel we were staying in, and it became my practice to find one slim hour each day when I knew she was either asleep or otherwise settled and secure when I could steal down there and just use the heck out of that pool. I'm not a big swimming enthusiast normally, but to slip under the water and be responsible for nothing but the movement of my limbs, to let the water hold me up—those feelings endure as my mental snapshot of release and self-care.

Likely as not, if you've been interested in reading this book, you are a person with the instinct to offer to hold the baby so the mama can pee alone or to sit with the patient so the spouse or offspring can go walk around the hospital parking lot. Most caregivers (though not all, it bears mentioning) will welcome an interlude of respite, and when we are one step removed we offer it because we recognize that it's a form of grace. The literature of caregiving is full of bitter lamentations from people tending to a sick or otherwise dependent person who felt abandoned by other relatives or their circle of friends, seemingly rendered invisible by the heavy air around the patient. The world of caregiving can feel like an odd, alternate universe, parallel to the Land of the Well but durably separate. Any bridge you can create between the two worlds will be as a lifeline to the recipient. As I said, a form of grace. Kudos to you if you take the chance to offer it.

Maybe you are the caregiver yourself, though. In that case, do you possibly need a reminder that you must replenish the well so it won't run dry? Because you must. You must do that.

There isn't always a pool in the basement, of course. Still, people committed to the care of others need a furlough of some kind. I felt selfish, leaving the room and leaving the idea of illness for that hour, because my sister couldn't. She couldn't take a day or even an hour off from her illness. But I had just enough willpower to take that swim, so I could come back to her somewhat restored to my task. That's all you need, as it turns out: just enough. Just enough willpower to go a little ways off, and just enough recharging to refresh you for the next stretch.

The situation is not always so dire and intense, of course. But the principle is a good one to fasten onto. It's hard to leave a parent's bedside or to place your colicky baby in the arms of your sister-in-law or to extract yourself from any situation where you feel essential. But if self-care doesn't motivate you in its purest sense, consider this: you have to attend to your own self if you want to stay on the plus side of the balance sheet. Flirting with (or heaven help us all, *encountering*) your own collapse adds nothing positive to the equation for the people you want to help.

It's a big square dance, this notion of care. To secure another person's oxygen mask, you must first apply your own. To extend yourself toward the care of another, you will need to receive a little grace from someone else. Person A can take care of Person B because Person C brought over dinner; Person C could make that dinner because she said yes when Person D offered to pick up her child from school. And so on, until the alphabet resets and you start the dance again.

The caregiver's break won't always be a spa day. Sometimes it will look less like a massage, mani-pedi, and seaweed wrap, and more like ten minutes with a book or in the shower or the outside air, or practicing scream therapy in the car. No matter if it's packed into a sliver of time or stretches over an afternoon, it's an essential item in the tool kit.

Whether you are providing this type of respite for yourself or another dear one, a tidy little uncomplicated meal of things that are straightforward and a little bit special, presented beautifully in a quiet space with something like good music playing or a funny thing to read, should be the goal state. If it has to be approximated on a park bench or in a bucket seat, so be it. Just keep respite and restoration in mind.

LEMON SOUP

Greeks are serious about lemons. I have collected hard data establishing that they are not comfortable leaving home, even to camp in the woods, with fewer than one lemon per person, per day. That they make a soup of lemons comes as no surprise, and I happily added that to my list of cultural comfort food appropriations.

SERVES 2 TO 4

For the
SOUP

2 cups chicken or
   vegetable stock
2 or 3 sprigs fresh mint
   or dill
2 or 3 strips lemon zest,
   removed with a carrot
   peeler

⅛ teaspoon Aleppo
   pepper, cayenne, or
   smoked paprika
Salt

For the
EGGY BUSINESS

1 egg, separated
¼ teaspoon salt
¼ teaspoon sugar

1 tablespoon lemon juice,
   strained of both pulp
   and seeds

For
SERVING

Freshly ground pepper
Excellent olive oil
Finely chopped fresh
   thyme, mint, or chives

1 To prepare the soup, bring the stock to a simmer in a large saucepan with the sprigs of fresh mint, lemon zest, and Aleppo pepper; taste and adjust for salt, with the understanding that the egg will tone it down some. Remove the stock from the heat and extract the solids. Set aside ½ cup of stock in a small cup.

2 Using a hand mixer, beat the egg white with the salt and sugar until soft peaks form.

3 Using a whisk, lightly beat the egg yolk and then gently fold it into the egg white, followed by the lemon juice.

4 Pour the reserved stock slowly into the lemon and egg mixture, whisking gently and continuously until all is incorporated. Return the soup pot to medium-low heat and whisk the lemon-egg mixture in. Simmer, whisking frequently, for about 15 minutes. The foam of the egg will mostly subside into the soup over this time, and the soup base will thicken slightly. You can skim the remaining foam or leave it; I find it delicious and amusing, and it makes a nice base for the little garnishes.

5 Garnish with a grind of pepper, a few drops of olive oil, and a scattering of fresh herbs.

ROASTED BROCCOLI

Roasting makes broccoli (and brussels sprouts, and all brassicas) insanely moreish, and when you involve lemons and salty crispy cheese, there's no stopping a person once they begin nibbling at the dish.

SERVES 1 TO 2

1 broccoli crown (about ½ pound)

1 tablespoon extra-virgin olive oil

1 teaspoon grated fresh ginger

Finely grated zest of ½ lemon

¼ teaspoon Aleppo pepper or crushed red pepper flakes

½ teaspoon kosher salt

1 tablespoon sliced almonds or pepitas

2–3 tablespoons freshly grated Parmesan or other hard, dry cheese

1 teaspoon lemon juice

1   Preheat the oven to 450°F, and line a sheet pan with parchment paper.

2   Trim the tough end off the broccoli, and peel the stalk. Break the florets apart and sliver the trunk into ½-inch sticks. Don't fuss over achieving regular sizes; variation makes for crispy bits.

3   Whisk together the oil, ginger, lemon zest, and Aleppo pepper in a large bowl. Add the broccoli and toss gently until evenly coated. Arrange the broccoli on the lined sheet pan, with enough distance between to allow for crisping, not steaming. Sprinkle with the salt.

4   Roast for 10–12 minutes. Remove the pan from the oven, flip the broccoli pieces, and scatter the almonds and Parmesan across the sheet pan.

5   Sprinkle the tray with the lemon juice and serve hot or at room temperature.

ACKNOWLEDGMENTS

I extend my loving thanks to many people for their help with this book:
Tom and Laura McNeal, who have rowed up in too many lifeboats to count or classify, always with just the right snacks.

Alana Chernila, for spoon butter and because cheese is delicious, the tips of two adjacent icebergs.

Naomi Blumenthal, Lauren Handel, Kari Harendorf, Amy Humes, Andrea Panaritis, and Julie Scott, for (among other gifts) the shelf-stable nourishment they create in the presence of apples.

Jenny Laird and Maria Sirois, for being sure this was going to happen and not really being interested in looking at it any other way.

Suzi Banks Baum, for firmly steering me toward the seat she had saved for me (and also for the mantra, "done is beautiful," and also for all the other things).

Alanna Taylor-Tobin, for practical wisdom and new old friendship, not in that order.

Marisa McClellan, Sara Moulton, and Julia Turshen for holding the door open.

Jennifer Urban-Brown and the team at Roost, and Jenny Stephens at Sterling Lord, for using their competent professional hands to soothe the feverish brow of an idea and grow it into a tidy volume (any remaining untidiness is mine, not theirs).

Amelia, Corie, Corinna, Elisa, Ginny, Jonathan, Lissa, Marni, Max, Me-mo, Papa, Pennie, Raphaela, and Sue, for testing recipes with thought and care and for waving the pom-poms, and all the regular readers and cheerleaders at *A Raisin & A Porpoise*, for reading and commenting. All of you made everything better.

Delta Bean, Bonzo, Rosa, and Sylvester: *You guys can't read!* As if that matters one iota.

My family (in all its extensions), for their hungers and their nutrients, and B, for enduring collaborations.

RESOURCES

CHAINS, TRAINS, AND AUTOMOBILES

Though ancient, the principle of sharing food between households is one that has benefited tremendously from technology. Websites abound now that make it a virtual snap to organize a meal train, communicate about dietary preferences and other details, and even orchestrate deliveries in cities beyond the reach of your kitchen.

MEAL TRAINS

Foodtidings.com
Lotsahelpinghands.com
Mealbaby.com
Mealtrain.com
Takethemameal.com

FOOD DELIVERY SERVICES

Bringmethat.com
Doordash.com
Grubhub.com

FURTHER READING

Alternative Baker: Reinventing Dessert with Gluten-Free Grains and Flours by Alanna Taylor-Tobin

Feed the Resistance: Recipes and Ideas for Getting Involved by Julia Turshen

Healing Wise by Susun S. Weed

Home Cooking: A Writer in the Kitchen and *More Home Cooking: A Writer Returns to the Kitchen* by Laurie Colwin

The Homemade Kitchen: Recipes for Cooking with Pleasure by Alana Chernila

Laurel's Kitchen Caring: Recipes for Everyday Home Caregiving by Laurel Robertson with Carol Lee Flinders and Brian Ruppenthal, RD

The Moosewood Cookbook (and others) by Mollie Katzen

Roald Dahl's Revolting Recipes by Roald and Felicity Dahl

A Short Course in Happiness After Loss by Maria Sirois

Ten Essential Herbs by Lalitha Thomas

Twelve Recipes by Cal Peternell

Veganomicon: The Ultimate Vegan Cookbook (and others) by Isa Chandra Moskowitz and Terry Hope Romero

GET ACTIVE

We build stronger communities when we make the effort to learn more about cultures beyond our own; firsthand experience of what we hold in common and what we can learn from one another enriches lives on both sides of a perceived divide. Food is such an efficient and effective (and pleasant!) means for making these kinds of connections, from person-to-person up to larger-scale change. Cross-cultural eating doesn't have to be limited to restaurant dining or the adventures you undertake in your home kitchen. If you are ready to reach outside your ken, here are a few resources to help you expand your horizons, lend a helping hand, and build a web of strength.

GO SHOPPING

Homeboyfoods.com
Hotbreadkitchen.org
Sunflowerbakery.org/shop

Hot Bread Kitchen is a New York City–based mail-order bakery offering over seventy-five multiethnic breads, inspired by the cultures of the women training in their bakery for careers in food service. Your purchase supports the training program as well as the business incubator they operate, and helps to preserve traditional baking techniques practiced around the world. Sunflower Bakery is a DC-area counterpart, and Homeboy Foods is a West Coast version. All ship nationally.

ORDER IN

With minimal research, I easily found catering companies, food trucks, bakeries, and other edible enterprises that focus on helping low-income, refugee and immigrant communities build futures for themselves and their families in just about every state in the US and across the globe. Use search terms like "refugee," "immigrant," or "low income," and then add "job training," and "food," "bakery," or "catering" to find places in your zip code where your food dollars can help support these efforts.

GET SCHOOLED

Lacocinasf.org
Leagueofkitchens.com
Localabundancekitchen.org

The League of Kitchens is an immersive culinary adventure in New York City where immigrants teach intimate cooking workshops in their homes. The mission of San Francisco–based La Cocina is to cultivate low-income food entrepreneurs from communities of color and immigrant communities by providing affordable commercial kitchen space, technical assistance, and market opportunities. Local Abundance Kitchen is a Cleveland-area organization that seeks to educate and assist refugees and immigrants by offering them a platform to teach cooking classes and workshops. It is highly likely a similar organization exists near you, if none of these are close by, or check with a local community center to explore (or host) an offering like it.

COME TO THE TABLE
Displacedkitchens.com
Komeeda.com/about
Thedinnerparty.org
Thepeoplessupper.org
Transformationtable.com

National, regional, and local organizations that encourage strangers to collect and connect at the table are popping up all over. Use any of these portals to connect to an event in your area, or start one of your own.

GET INVOLVED
Foodnotbombs.net
Nokidhungry.org

Food justice organizations that seek to redistribute surplus food and address hunger in America exist from the grassroots level, working upward to bigger organizations that partner with corporations to reach very wide. Find your match and lend your dollars, hours, and other muscle to helping them get it done.

INDEX

ABOUT THE AUTHOR

Janet Reich Elsbach lives in rural western Massachusetts. A graduate of Stanford University, she also holds a master's degree in education from New York University. She teaches writing to adults with developmental disabilities, and for fifteen years was a counselor to new and growing families. She writes about how all the numerous things going on in the average life collide with making dinner on her blog, *A Raisin & A Porpoise*. She has chased strange ingredients, healing nutrition, and good food all her life, and now it has come to this.